By Gloria Vanderbilt

◄══►

IT SEEMED IMPORTANT AT THE TIME

A Romance Memoir

GLORIA VANDERBILT

SIMON & SCHUSTER
New York   London   Toronto   Sydney

Illustration credits appear on page 162.

SIMON & SCHUSTER
Rockefeller Center
1230 Avenue of the Americas
New York, NY 10020

SIMON & SCHUSTER and colophon are registered
trademarks of Simon & Schuster, Inc.

For information about special discounts for bulk purchases,
please contact Simon & Schuster Special Sales:
1-800-456-6798 or business@simonandschuster.com

Designed by Joel Avirom

Photography Consultant: Kevin Kwan

Manufactured in the United States of America

1   3   5   7   9   10   8   6   4   2

Library of Congress Cataloging-in-Publication Data

Vanderbilt, Gloria, 1924-
   It seemed important at the time : a romance memoir / Gloria Vanderbilt.
      p. cm.
      1. Vanderbilt, Gloria, 1924- 2. Celebrities—United States—Biography.
3. Artists—United States—Biography. 4. Socialites—United States—Biography.
5. Actors—United States—Biography. 6. Women fashion designers—United
States—Biography. 7. Women designers—United States—Biography. I. Title.

CT275.V234A3 2004
700'.92—dc22

[B] 2004049146

ISBN 0-7432-6480-0

To Joyce Carol Oates

CONTENTS

⬌

Like a pack of tarot cards
haphazardly thrown out on a table—
pick one, turn it over, turn the page . . .

PREFACE

I've lived a lot, lost a lot, had dreams of love and fateful encounters, and although I suspect the answer is in the seeker, I still believe that what I'm looking for is just around the corner. Maybe it is. Why not? The phone can ring and your whole life can change. My life has been a roller coaster of ups and downs, highs and lows—one day caviar, next day a chocolate bar as the song says. I was born in a castle, but now, like Rapunzel in the fairy tale, I'm letting down my hair and telling you how it really was. But where to begin? Not at the beginning—that's no fun. Nor at the end, because my story is far from over.

Shall I start with scandal, or broken dreams? With great love, or shattering loss? I know now that you can't have one without the other. I could start with Howard Hughes or Frank Sinatra, men who came along at just the right moment. Or perhaps I should start with Truman Capote and his Black and White Ball, or the night I found a Bible in his bathroom, the pages cut to form a hollowed-out box that was filled with cocaine.

There have been so many people, so many moments. It's an ongoing education. I won't bore you with wisdom, clichés, or advice. Take what you want, and learn what you can. In the end, it's all any of us can do.

What can I say? I've lived and loved the way I have. I could have done it differently, I suppose, but there's no real point in regretting. What was important then is less so now, but I embrace it all: the pain and the pleasure, the drama and the disappointments . . . All of it seemed important at the time.

IT SEEMED
IMPORTANT
AT THE
TIME

ROMANCE

⇌

In romance what do you seek? Something new and Other, although you don't quite know what it is? For me romance is a yearning not fully conscious, but what I find is always the search for something else, a renewal and a hope for transformation. The creative risk-taking of passionate love not only gives you the chance to change the past, it gives the imagination one more chance at an exciting future.

THE SCARLET STING
OF SCANDAL

I find sex endlessly interesting. I suppose I always will. It's all in the head, of course; I realize that now. What we like, what we want, what we think we need is generated somewhere in that curious cortex of ours, created by the firing of synapses—the electricity of love.

I'd had no knowledge of sex as a child. We are talking about the 1930s, after all. Not exactly the Dark Ages, but not much better. The only "sex education" any of us had in those days was talking about it with other girls in school. Mentioning sex to grown-ups? Inconceivable.

My cousin Whitty and I were caught one summer by his governess fondling each other under a tent we'd innocently put up on the lawn right in front of my aunt Gertrude's bedroom window. I must have been about twelve. Needless to say, the tent was taken down, but the memory remained. How could anything that felt so good be bad?

Later, I was sent to Miss Porter's School in Farmington, Connecticut, where my best friend was a hefty, jovial extrovert who reminded me oddly of my Irish nanny, Dodo. Wanting to be liked is fatal, though it would take me years to learn that. I wanted desperately to please my friend, and was willing to try anything to make her happy.

During one vacation, we found ourselves in bed at Aunt Gertrude's house on Fifth Avenue. The structure, designed by William Schickel in the early 1880s, was as large as Grand Central Terminal and about as cozy. My friend had come for the Easter holiday, and each night would tippy-toe from her room down the cold marble halls right into my bed. I couldn't wait. We'd cuddle in the huge canopied four-poster and, well, have at it. Truth be told, it was great. Of course, I didn't quite know what *it* was, but whatever *it* was, I didn't want it to stop.

By the time we got back to school, it was over. Frankly, it had gone a little too far, and I had gotten scared. A few weeks later, at nearby Avon School, two boys were expelled. Their crime? It was never announced, of course, but whispers spread like wildfire. *Homosexuality.*

I hadn't a clue what the word meant, but judging by the way everyone reacted, I knew it was a scandal. It didn't take me long to figure out that what they had done was probably not too different than what my friend and I had done in my aunt's four-poster bed, and when I realized that, my heart stopped. This was not the first time I'd heard such whispers—not the first time I'd felt the sting of such a scandal.

A few years before, at the age of ten, I had been at the center of a custody battle between my mother and my father's sister, Gertrude Vanderbilt Whitney. At the time it was called the trial of the century. I suppose each generation likes to claim that dubious distinction. Since then there have been many far more important court cases, but at the time it caused quite a stir.

If I may digress for a moment: The first time I saw Judge Judy on her TV show *Open Court* I was mesmerized, and couldn't stop imagining my custody case being tried in her court. My Aunt Gertrude—tall, thin, so elegant in her fedora, so ice-cold in her reserve—would be no match for the diminutive Judge Judy, nor would my grandmother Naney Morgan, clutching rosary beads, flashing her mahogany lacquered nails, her orange hair, unleashing her venom as she testified against my mother. Then along would come Dodo, my nanny, so fat, so solid, so scared that she wasn't going to follow Aunt Gertrude's lawyer's instructions. And then the star: my Mummy, exquisite in her black dress, so passive, so bewildered, twisting her plover's-egg-size diamond engagement ring, wondering what it was all about. Judge Judy wouldn't subject me to the hostile formality of the witness stand. Instead I'd be invited up to sit beside her on the bench for a cozy chat—so she could get a sense of what I was like, and what *I* wanted.

But at the time, I had no such luck. Judge Judy hadn't even been born. I bring up the custody battle because in the midst of the trial, my mother's maid testified on the stand that she had seen my mother in bed kissing the Lady Milford-Haven. As a very young child I had known Lady Milford-Haven in England and she lingered somewhere in my mind's eye, a grown-up with a halo of red hair, hands with jeweled rings, clothed in brilliant hues, always laughing in fun when she and my Mummy were together—yes, I remembered her well, had been fascinated by her, but at the same time somehow threatened, excluded. "Nada," which is diminutive for Nadeja, married Prince George of Battenburg, whose mother was a granddaughter of Queen Victoria. After the First World War, the house of Battenburg assumed by royal decree the new name of Milford-Haven. Prince George's aunt was the ill-

fated czarina of Russia, and he was first cousin of King George. Nada's father, the Grand Duke Michael, was also related to the royal house of England. And now this testimony was so shocking that the court was instantly closed. *Lesbian*—the word, like blood, was splashed over the tabloids, branding my mother with a scarlet letter.

But at the time, I didn't even know the court had been closed. While the world outside was in the Great Depression, and followed the trial daily in the tabloids, I was cloistered at Aunt Gertrude's estate in Old Westbury, Long Island, where life went on as if nothing had happened. Her estate, a kingdom unto itself, was screened against the outside by detectives and minions working for her. Newspapers were banned. I overheard grandmother Naney Morgan and my nanny whispering about something DARK and TERRIBLE, something that "the little one mustn't hear." My Chilean grandmother had a gift for histrionics—her eyes would roll up in her head, and she'd slide into her native Spanish, propelled by rage against my mother. Yes, there was a DARK and TERRIBLE secret about my mother.

It was at school, at Farmington, when I realized for the first time that what those boys had done with each other, what I had done with my friend, had something in common with my mother and the energetic Lady Milford-Haven. The realization terrified me. I wanted to be good, and to please people and have them love me; they wouldn't if they found out the *sin* I had committed—a sin I'd never dare confess even to the priest or anyone else. I was convinced I could never again receive the holy Sacrament, never be saved from "original sin." I didn't know what "original sin" was, but the priests were always talking about it, so I assumed it was important.

A scarlet letter—*Lesbian*—publicly branded on my mother, would hover as a shadow over me, and the humiliation she experienced haunted me for years. That gentle, passive creature, who never understood one single thing that really happened to her . . . It took me a long time to resolve the feelings I had about her bisexuality, and until I did, there was the hovering fear that I might be like her. In my head I knew there would be nothing wrong in that, but knowing and believing are two different things. Years later, walking in New York on Madison Avenue, a young man said "Hello," only it wasn't a young man, it was my Farmington best friend, whom I hadn't seen since then. I was so terrified I'd be drawn to her, I hurried by pretending I didn't even know her.

Would any of this have mattered today? Perhaps, but not as much as it did in 1933. Thank goodness it's different now. Same-sex couples can be loving parents, not just by adopting a child but by giving birth. I believe it's only a matter of time before they have all the rights that heterosexual couples do. And why the hell shouldn't they? Love is love.

I have always respected women more than men. Or perhaps I should say I've always understood women more than I have men. It's a cliché, of course, but men truly are a mystery. Even now, I haven't a clue as to how they think or what goes on in their minds. Really, it wasn't until I resolved my relationship with my mother and came to understand her that I stopped feeling competitive with men, threatened by them. I suppose I had always seen them as the enemy. I suppose if I'd been a lesbian, it might have been easier, but it just didn't turn out that way. I have made some men miserable—although never intentionally—and I've made a lot of men happy. A favorable balance in the end.

And despite the scandal I've known, the mistakes I've made and sometimes repeated, I still wake each day believing the next great thing, the next great love, is just around the corner. Falling in love is an act of the imagination, and my imagination is stronger than ever.

LITTLE RED RIDING HOOD AND THE BIG BAD WOLVES

I can't remember the first time I started to notice boys.
I can't recall the exact moment they came into the
picture. But when they did, nothing was ever the same
again. Boys, boys, boys. Heady stuff, I can tell you. And
they liked *me*. Having low self-esteem, it made me think
maybe there was something lovable about me after all.
I had flirted with the idea of becoming a nun, but once
boys came into the picture, being a nun didn't seem like
such a great idea. God was one thing, boys another.

I was strictly chaperoned, of course, though it
seems so foreign now. In those days, there were subdeb
parties at the Waldorf, and tea dancing at The Plaza; it was
Glenn Miller and moonlight serenades. That was New York
just before the war. When I was seventeen, I went out to
California for what was supposed to be a two-week visit
with my mother. It felt like I had arrived in heaven.

In the summer of 1941, my Mummy lived with her twin sister, Thelma, whom I called Aunt Toto, in a house on Maple Drive in Beverly Hills. Thelma was having an affair with actor Edmund Lowe, whom she called "Edmond" in the French manner, and if they weren't out, they were in her room with the door shut. When I arrived I was told Mummy was having some sort of nervous something or other. She drifted around the garden saying she had "cancer," and sat at her dressing table, gazing in the mirror, threatening to dye her dark hair blond. She popped pills called Luminal and had a crystal decanter of brandy on her night table with a pretty crystal glass next to it. She spent most of her time with a woman named Kitty, a terrifying extrovert who wore an unfortunate blond wig. Kitty had been in the movies, but nobody seemed to know which ones.

What I most wanted to do when I arrived in California was to date movie stars. It felt unreal, arriving in Hollywood, basically on my own after the grip my Aunt Gertrude had on me in Old Westbury—*strict,* you better believe it. Suddenly, the door of the cage was open, and out I flew, into the nights of Beverly Hills. Catch me if you can!

The first actor I met was Van Heflin, and we became "engaged" almost immediately. He had appeared on Broadway with Katharine Hepburn in *Philadelphia Story,* and she'd been my role model ever since I saw her in the movie *Little Women,* so I thought he was quite a catch. Excitedly I wrote Cathleen, my half sister, swearing her to secrecy and telling her that Van and I were going house-hunting the very next day. She passed this bit of news instantly on to Aunt Gertrude, who had a fit. A fit! But what could she do about it? Nothing.

In her fuzzy-wuzzy way, Mummy seemed enthusiastic about my "engagement" to Van. "I was married at eighteen," she murmured with a delicate little one-sided smile. Needless to say, our "engagement" soon dissolved, disappearing into the wild blue yonder without a trace. No worry, there were others waiting in the wings.

It Seemed Important at the Time

Every night I was dancing at Ciro's with actors all much older than me. A young man I had been mad about in New York now seemed a callow youth, a boy. Now it was actors: Errol Flynn, George Montgomery, or Bruce Cabot, later known to me around the gaming table as "Cousin Brucie." I'd dine with one of them at Romanoffs, then be on to Mocambo with someone else.

Then, huffing and puffing one afternoon at the Beverly Hills Hotel pool, along came Pasquale De Cicco; everyone called him Pat. He wasn't an actor, but he looked like one—knock-over handsome, in style and personality very much like the singer/actor Dean Martin. True, he wasn't much in the brain department, but he did have a flair for gin rummy, and he was funny in his way. He'd walk into a room and have everyone laughing at his sophomoric repartee. I never opened my mouth, just tried to look pretty in pink—how could nothing me have anything to say? Why did I want to attract his attention? Why did I want to impress him? Why did I feel better about myself when I did? Did it have to do with fascination with his flashy extroverted glamour, which was so completely the opposite of myself? Or was it some kind of chemistry, and who can explain that?

His father was known as the Broccoli King, having, it was said, brought broccoli to this country from Italy. Well, my grandmother Naney Morgan did always favor royalty. Pat worked for Howard Hughes, whom I hadn't met, doing exactly what, nobody seemed to know. Mostly he hung around the pool at the Beverly Hills Hotel, playing gin rummy with Bruce Cabot, an agent named Charlie Feldman, and Joe Schenk, the head of Twentieth Century–Fox, whom everybody called "Uncle Joe." It was boring beyond belief. I mainly lolled around in the sun, waiting for Pat to pay me some attention. "Uncle Joe" took me aside once and leered at me: "I know what it is gets you about Pat." "What?" I said, puzzled. "The hair on his chest." "Ugh!" I winced.

The Hollywood Reporter had labeled this group "The Wolf Pack," which I suppose made me one of the Little Red Riding Hoods, something I didn't like one bit. Still, when Pat asked me for a date to go dancing at Mocambo I didn't say no. Afterward, I was all shaky inside wondering if he would ask me out again. Sadly, he did.

THE GREAT THING

O ne day an unexpected call came for my Mummy.
She was all atwitter and had come back to life again.
Wannsie, her devoted lady's maid, rummaged through her
closet, bringing out dresses to help her decide what to
wear. Finally one of her velvet tea gowns was selected, the
claret-color one with long sleeves that made her look, with
her long waving hair, like a Burne-Jones Pre-Raphaelite
heroine. It turned out that all the scurrying around was for
Howard Hughes—he was coming for tea. The call had
come out of nowhere. They had never met, but he
introduced himself on the phone and asked "could he
come to see her?" There was something he wanted to talk
to her about. "I wonder what it can be," she murmured,
gazing at herself in the mirror as Wannsie attached her
stockings to her garter belt.

I was going out as Hughes was coming in—a tall
stranger, handsome as a movie star. Anyway, it turned out
it was me, not Mummy, whom he had taken a fancy to.
He came to ask her permission to give me a screen test?

Gloria Vanderbilt

Me—a movie star! Yes, why not! Maybe that would be THE GREAT THING.

Mummy wasn't too taken with Howard's proposal. She took off the velvet gown and went back to bed, listening to music on the radio until Kitty tooted by in her car and took her away somewhere across the border to Mexico or to Cal Neva for the weekend—who knows? Thelma and Edmund, at least, were amused by the screen test notion. I wasn't amused. I was *thrilled,* and not only thrilled, but dead serious, because while I had wanted to be a nun when I grew up, my alternate plan was to be an actress, a famous movie star. On one occasion I even got up the nerve to mention something along those lines to Aunt Gertrude—the actress part, not the rest of it—but the idea didn't grab her. So I retreated back into my mound of baby fat; there were lots of fat nuns around, even though they weren't famous. You may think you'd like to be famous, don't you? But in what way? Of course by the time I went out to Hollywood there was no more baby fat to contend with, and here I was at last on the brink of stardom—all it would take was my fateful meeting with Howard Hughes. Yes, yes, *it* was waiting for me just around the corner.

Not long to wait. I agonized over what to wear for the date with Howard—spent endless time preparing— long soak in Adena Fluffy Bubble Milk Bath, bubbles

Gloria Vanderbilt

surging up from the powerful force of the water, foaming into clouds of heavenly white over my gorgeous body, like blobs of egg white on my favorite dessert, Floating Island. Isn't beauty an adventure? Yes, I was floating in an island of snow—only the snow was warm and soft-scented—and when I closed my eyes, I dreamed of stardom.

Wannsie came in with a silver goblet of Dry Sack sherry shaken up into a frosty amber cocktail. She placed it beside me on the ledge of the tub and said, "What are you wearing tonight, Miss Gloria?"

I took a sip. "Oh, I don't know—maybe the new green."

Wannsie trotted over to the closet and picked something green out from the many dresses and put it on the bed for me to contemplate as I floated back into the bath's fluffiness. I kept wishing that I could show myself off to Mummy, have *her* see how I looked when I was all dressed up. She would think I was pretty and maybe even admire me.

It seems so long ago. I wanted a family, of course, but I also dreamed of fame and wanted Howard's magic wand to tap me on the shoulder. Not that "fame" hadn't already tapped me, so to speak. I was born into a well-known American family and then, later, at age ten had survived the infamous custody case. Yes, I already had fame, but was famous for what? Nothing of merit. The only fame that impressed me, the only fame that mattered, was fame for what you achieved by your talents. That's why actors dazzled me. Artists did, too. They were famous for a reason, and therefore worthy. I wasn't worthy, but someday I would be. Quite how I didn't yet know— but I was *determined*.

For my date with Howard I ended up wearing a Lanz of Salzburg peasant skirt and blouse, and I dabbed tons of Schiaparelli Shocking perfume behind my ears. The blouse was white cotton with a square neck and black velvet ribbon running through its ruffled décolletage, and the skirt was ruffled too, quite costumey, and the rage that summer. The only thing not good about it—too young, it made me look too young. I studied myself in the mirror. Yes, definitely, much too young. Maybe put a gray streak in my hair? But it was too late for that, because the doorbell rang and it was *him*—Howard Hughes, waiting with his magic wand.

Today it's hard to erase the image we have in our minds of what Howard Hughes became at the end of his life—the long unkempt beard, the man in isolation in Las Vegas on the top floor of the Sands Hotel, rumors of behavior so bizarre it went way beyond eccentricity. What was he really like? All I can tell you is how he was when I knew him that summer. Beyond that, I can only guess at the strange demons that possessed him, turning him into

Gloria Vanderbilt

the paranoiac recluse he apparently became. There was nothing when I knew him to suggest what lay ahead. Wannsie had let him in and there he was, waiting in Mummy's living room as I flew down the stairs and into his life.

In the days that followed I saw a lot of him. Sometimes he would pick me up and we'd just drive toward Malibu; the radio would play soft music, and we talked. I was shy and he was, too. He was also slightly deaf and spoke in a voice so low that sometimes you'd have to lean close to hear him. I tried to tell him about my aunt and my mother and how I felt about what happened, but since I didn't really know myself I'd get lost in a maze of confusion and end up saying, "Oh, I'll tell you another time," and I'd end up sitting silently on the seat beside him, looking out at the Pacific Ocean rolling by.

Once we stopped to pick up a hitchhiker. Something about the young man was touching as he stood there alone in the road. Howard stopped the car and we drove to Robinson's where he bought him an outfit—suit, shoes, and shirt.

While Howard was paying the bill, the young man, stunned by it all, said to me, "Who *is* he?"

"Santa Claus," I whispered with a smile.

We met at offbeat times—I'd get a call saying John (an assistant) would pick me up at Maple Drive at eleven;

John would then drive me in one car to meet Howard in his car parked on a side road somewhere. Off we'd go to have pancakes at a diner. Other times I found myself at his house, a haphazardly furnished place with dust sheets over most of the furniture, and a recording of the "Moonlight Sonata" playing somewhere (to this day I can never hear it without thinking of him). Some evenings he worked at Lockheed while I watched a movie in his private screening room until he came in, and we'd have dinner right there, as if we were on a picnic. He always ate the same things, whether there or in a restaurant—steak, peas, and a baked potato—so I always had that, too.

Howard was serious, very, unlike anyone I'd ever met. After being with him, suddenly the razzle-dazzle of Hollywood didn't seem important anymore, and the famous grown-up actors too had lost their glamour. One night he screened *Hell's Angels,* which he was especially proud of since it was the first movie he produced and directed. It starred Jean Harlow; she had been one of his discoveries.

Sometimes we flew to Catalina. "Look down," he said. "See the pattern the lights make on the dark land? That's one way to tell what city you're over." It was like looking at a pattern of stars, only they were below us and not above.

In Catalina, Howard would land the plane and

we'd walk along the beach. Once a woman with a camera recognized him and came up to ask if she could take our picture. He didn't like that idea at all and pulled me away quickly down the beach.

I never for a moment thought Howard was eccentric or strange in the way he did things. Quite the contrary: I loved his spontaneity and the surprise of it, and suddenly I didn't feel shy with him anymore. He was very *real* about everything, and that's when I realized I had lost all my dreams of him making me a famous movie star. All I wanted was for him to love me. But of course, it wasn't to be. Or perhaps it was, but I didn't realize it at the time, and so it never was.

Even after I met Howard Hughes and stopped seeing anyone else, I'd hear that Pat De Cicco was dating starlets like pretty Betty Avery and feel jealous. When Pat called me again, and asked me to "Uncle Joe" Schenk's for Sunday lunch by the pool, I said no, but it came out yes, and there I was, back as I was before, waiting around to have Pat pay me some attention. Howard didn't like it when I saw Pat again, and said he'd send Pat to Dallas to take care of catering for TWA.

"Oh God, yes—do—do do that, please get him out of the way," I said. But why wasn't I secure enough to just tell Pat to get out of the way myself? Pat was, of course, all wrong. There were his unpredictable mood swings, when his temper would flare without reason, striking out at whoever was handy. But there was something else, too—his first wife, actress Thelma Todd, had been killed in an unsolved murder, and there were rumors . . .

Some women are drawn to men in prison, criminals they don't know, and they start corresponding, forming a "relationship," romanticizing that she is all he needs to change him, transform him into Prince Charming. I heard myself telling Pat that I was *upset* Howard was banishing him to Siberia. Why did I say this when all I wanted *was* to get him out of town? Before he left he got a lot off his hairy chest—things about Howard Hughes—"Listen, stupido" (one of his pet names for me), "what makes you think you're different from all his other girls?" He shouted, and words were flung around like stones—"girl girls," "movie stars," "marriage," "left at altar," "Who do you think *you* are, fatso." All of which made me believe that Howard could never, ever, really be serious about wanting to marry me.

Then word came from Aunt Gertrude: a message from her feared lawyer, the hated Mr. Crocker, demanding that I go back to New York. This time it was a command, backed up by Surrogate Foley, my legal guardian—a summons that couldn't be ignored. So yes, Mummy, Kitty, and I flew back on a TWA plane. On the nine-hour flight they were like schoolgirls on a picnic, drinking lemonade

Gloria Vanderbilt

spiked with gin, giggling at private jokes. More and more, as the summer went on, they were really getting to me. They were even getting to Aunt Thelma. "*What* am I going to do about your mother?" she'd say from time to time. God knows I didn't have the answers. But then Edmund would be coming to pick her up for lunch at Romanoffs, and she became preoccupied with which John Frederics hat to wear.

We were booked on the flight incognito under the name of Vane to avoid publicity, and it was a kick when "Miss Vane" was invited up front to meet captain and crew (arranged by Howard, of course), a kick walking into the cockpit, as if I had walked into the intricate insides of a watch. But it was even more of a kick when I found Katharine Hepburn on the same flight. She who had been a shadowy role model seen only on the distant silver screen in *Little Women,* cavorting around in the snow, confidently throwing snowballs at her chum Laurie, was now present, here on this very plane, breathing the same air I was. Hadn't Howard been in love with her? How could I ever compete with someone like that? I mustered all the courage I could and left Mummy and Kitty, slipping invisibly into the empty seat facing Hepburn. But instead of getting a good look at her, I was too polite and only stared, transfixed, out the window until I chickened out completely and went back to my seat where I prayed to God that *she* wouldn't see Mummy and Kitty and their shenanigans.

Freddy, Aunt Gertrude's chauffeur, met me at the airport in the familiar gray Rolls-Royce and drove me back to Old Westbury. It was weird. Where was the girl who left here all those years ago—only it wasn't years, it was just a few months. We drove along winding roads into the forest until there we were, in front of that house I knew so well, the house where so many things had happened. Only now it wasn't home. "Home," such as it was, was now the elusive Mummy, and Maple Drive, was now Mocambo/Romanoffs/Ciro's, where every time I arrived the doorman would say "Welcome home." It was Thelma and Edmund behind the closed door. It was Kitty talking brassy and laughing as she fussed with the unfortunate wig. It was Mummy and Kitty calling from somewhere on the phone in the middle of the night, scaring me, saying they heard I was taking marijuana (what was that?). "Home" was Pat and "Uncle Joe" and the damn gin rummy. It was Howard's beat-up Packard and a plane flying to Catalina.

Outside the front door, as always, stood the pair of statues of white and black spotted Dalmatians, and there was butler William opening the door, and inside, Aunt Gertrude waiting in her creamy cashmere and silk pant outfit, pearls at wrist and neck, soft fedora with feather, for she usually wore a hat even in the house. I dressed for the occasion, as grown-up as I could be, in spike Delman heels, Arden's shocking-pink lipstick and a black Howard Greer dress just like one Rita Hayworth had.

I dreaded seeing Aunt Gertrude again, but her manners, as always, were superb. (Do you think that gracious manners are bred, or learned?) There was a jigsaw puzzle she'd been working on, and after she embraced me (coolly), she leaned over and put a piece in place. "I have something to suggest," she said. "Why don't you marry Geoff and come back to live here with me?"

Geoff was the young man in New York I had been besotted with. I would have died to hear this before I went to visit Mummy in Hollywood. He was the first boy I loved, and we were crazy to get married after he graduated from Princeton that spring. But now it seemed like baby talk.

"You can have any kind of wedding you'd like," she went on.

I don't care about him anymore, I told her. I'm in love with Howard Hughes and he's in love with me, I blurted out. I had already informed my old nanny, Dodo, of this fact, and it knocked her socks off. She had already bought a silver medal enameled with a Virgin Mary and had it engraved on the back, "G.V. to H.H. July 1941." She sent it to me to give him, but I didn't think he was all that religious, so I hadn't.

IT SEEMED IMPORTANT AT THE TIME

That first night of sleeping in my old room was strange. My school clothes still hung in the closet, just as I left them. And the white eyelet lace dress I'd been so thrilled to wear to the Piping Rock Club dance the week before I left for Hollywood—how babyish it looked now. This was the room I had called mine since I came to live with Aunt Gertrude when I was nine. It had been her husband Harry Payne Whitney's room, and never redecorated—a man's room, a mahogany room. None of that had changed. The view out the window—the green lawn stretching down into the meadows beyond—was still there, as it had always been. Yes, everything was the same. It was only me that had changed.

Sometime during the night I went down the long hall to Aunt Gertrude's room and stood outside her door. Did I intend to knock? Would she answer? Would I dare? I could hear her coughing, and I wanted to bring her a glass of water, but instead went back to my room and lay awake until dawn, waiting to get out out out, and back back back—but to what?

The hell about being in a cage is that you don't have choices. But since living at Mummy's, I not only had choices, I had too many choices, so many it was completely out of hand. Where should I go now? I wondered. Mummy was no help, and "suggestions" from Aunt Gertrude would have me right back where I was before, locked up tight in a room. I wanted to be free, free of the whole damn lot of them. But how? When? It would be four years until I turned twenty-one and could lay claim to the money I inherited, so *that* had no reality for me. Going back to school to finish my senior year and graduate might not have been such a bad idea, but my education had somehow disappeared into a crack, and the thought of facing the dreaded math and the confines of school never came up as an option. And college? Aunt Gertrude wasn't

It Seemed Important at the Time

gung-ho on college, so it was never in the picture. And as for my Mummy, she was in agreement with Gertrude. After all, hadn't she, after a sketchy month or so of school at the Sacred Heart Convent, married my father?

The next morning I went back to New York, to my mother, who was staying at the St. Regis. There were yellow roses and phone calls waiting for me from Howard, even a letter written on yellow lined paper (I still have it) saying he missed me and spent dinners alone, "pushing the peas around on the plate." When was I coming back? he asked. I didn't know when, or what was going to happen. I was jittery, kept looking in the mirror, but nobody was there. Pat was right. How could I possibly ever think I'd be worthy of someone like Howard? Or anyone else for that matter.

And then suddenly, unexpectedly, there was Pat in New York, yakety-yakking away at the King Cole Bar in the St. Regis, keeping the table in stitches, but cutting me dead when I caught his eye. You could tell he was mad mad *mad*, really angry, because he had figured out why he spent those weeks toiling away for TWA in Dallas at some catering job trumped up by Howard to get him out of town and away from me. He was dark as thunder and I longed for him to look at me again and smile and like me and love me. It didn't take long.

The next evening we were dancing the night away at El Morocco with Rita Hayworth and her husband, Eddie Judson, in town for some publicity stuff. She sat there silent and gorgeous as a Barbie doll, never opening her mouth. Just like me, only I didn't think I was gorgeous; I was trying desperately to be grown-up, or if not *be*, at least *look* that way. I wanted to talk with Mummy about what was happening with Pat and Howard, but her "cancer" had come back again, not to mention her preoccupation with the hair-color problem. And there was a puzzling little note left on my pillow at the St. Regis, which I found at dawn when I got back from Pat and El Morocco: "May you always be as happy as you are now—Love, Mummy." (Good God!) What did that mean? So I tried talking to my best friend, Carol Marcus, about Pat, but all she came up with was, "Ooo—but he's sooo like Heathcliff." But then she said that too about the raucous William Saroyan, whom she would soon marry. So what did she know? I was confused, panicked and uncertain about everything—everything, that is, but one decision. I couldn't go back to living with my mother, and I wasn't going back to live with Aunt Gertrude. Best get married. Quick. And I did—not to Howard, but to Pat. The Big Bad Wolf.

WEDDED BLISS . . .

$$\longleftrightarrow$$

It seemed important at the time to appear grown-up, much older than my seventeen years. Wouldn't the fact that I was married make it so?

Living with Pat was like walking on a tightrope, never knowing what would set him off on one of his violent spells when for no apparent reason he'd turn and vent his anger on his longing-to-please, docile wife, who was living off his smile while trying to keep her balance. To give you an idea of these charming scenes: Once, when we were staying at the Muelbach Hotel in Kansas City, the breakfast table was wheeled in by a friendly waiter. Pat, dripping wet from the shower, padded out, ordering the waiter to pour the coffee. He had a towel draped around him, but when he tasted the coffee he suddenly turned furious at the waiter. "This is mule piss," he shouted, taking the towel from around his waist and whipping it across the table so that the buckwheat pancakes and the poached eggs, the sticky maple syrup—

everything went spinning onto the floor. Then, as an afterthought, he hurled the table sideways after it.

It was a hoot, I can tell you. I wanted to follow the waiter as he ran from the room, but knew if I did I'd pay for it later. Best to keep silent and ride it out, even though I knew he'd blame me for the "mule piss" coffee. Then he looked down at the floor and seemed to come back into the reality of the room from some dark place, surprised at the havoc he had wrought.

Gloria Va
and Pasq
DiCicco i

I never told my friends about these episodes. I was too ashamed. Can you understand that? Too ashamed that I had married a man who would behave as he did.

Another time, alone, going to meet him at the Fort Riley Army Base in Junction City, Kansas, where he was in officer training camp, I overheard an older man and his son sitting beside me on the train talking, and suddenly they started gossiping about me and Pat. They, of course, did not recognize me, and had no idea that I was overhearing their conversation.

To my horror I heard the young man say, "How could she marry that gigolo?"

Why indeed? But I was stung to the quick, sitting silently as they went on and on . . .

Soon the train arrived at our destination and they stood behind me as we filed off the train. In a few minutes I would disappear into the crowd, the sting still mine alone. I took a deep breath, turned and looked them straight in the eyes, and, heart pounding, said, "I'm Gloria Vanderbilt." They were so floored, it was as if I had socked them in the stomach. I felt the surge of a small victory. Alone, I stood up for myself. But in my secret heart I always knew I could.

HAPPY BIRTHDAY

Fame casts a long shadow, is mysterious, inaccessible, transforming a famous person into something that usually has nothing to do with who the person really is.

An image of Leopold Stokowski was blazed in my mind's eye years before we met. Remember, in the movie *Fantasia,* when he's conducting the Philadelphia Orchestra and Mickey Mouse walks up to the podium to attract his attention? That's how I first saw Leopold. An archangel with a halo of white, and hands waving around, bringing forth sounds, pulling me right up to heaven with him. He seems at first so unattainable. But *lo!* he speaks, sounds actually come forth as he bends down to shake hands with Mickey. Is he part human after all? When I first saw the movie I may have been Mickey Mouse myself, but on that fateful night when I first met Stokowski at a party in Manhattan I was a mouse no longer. I was twenty years old, sexy, and it was a whole other story. No doubt about it.

I knew the marriage with Pat was over, but a week before he was to be shipped overseas he became ill with septicemia and was saved by a new drug, penicillin, and discharged from the Army. This put him in a cheery mood, free once again to pursue gin games and nights at El Morocco. It was just like old times in Hollywood, only it was New York, where we were staying at my cousin Sonny Whitney's apartment in the River House, and the cast had changed. It was now Hal Sims, Dan Topping, and Lex Thompson at the gaming table, set up permanently in the golden-green library overlooking the East River. The smoke-filled sessions continued day and night, night and day. I finally had had enough. Have you any idea the pleasure it was for me to tell him to take his pack of cards and scram—vamoose—out out out? No more fear of violent tempers, black eyes, head-banging against walls, and so on. I knew now that if necessary I was perfectly capable of "KO'ing" him (ummm—is that the correct term?) in the first round. Grandmother Naney Morgan pounced in with Dodo close behind, urging that I get an annulment. I easily could have, because we had been married in the Roman Catholic Church and he hadn't told me he couldn't have children. But I didn't give this idea a thought. I wanted it over right away.

Where was my Mummy during all of this? Alas, nowhere. No, my Mummy had been out of it almost since Leopold Stokowski came into it—ever since the surprise party I hastily planned to introduce my beautiful Mummy

to *Him*. While making
these arrangements I
practically had to put a
muzzle on to keep from
shouting my exciting
news from the Empire
State Building. Yes! The
very thing—a surprise
party for my Mummy
and all my friends with
Him as the mystery guest.
Has anyone truly
surprised or astonished
you? Negatively?
Positively? Well, I
certainly surprised my

Mummy. Atwitter with love we made our entrance, aglitter
and aglow, yes—and my Mummy almost fell on the floor.
She appeared totally and utterly flabbergasted.

There I stood with Him beside me, not only the
world-famous orchestra conductor, more controversial than
Arturo Toscanini, but aside from everything else, he'd had an
affair with Greta Garbo, whom my Mummy ecstatically
admired—that alone would knock her socks off, or so I
thought. Could it be that it may even have had something to
do with my wanting to attract him? (Gloria—please!) My

It Seemed Important at the Time

mother was stunned, and I just couldn't figure out why. It seemed to have something to do with my being twenty and he sixtysomething, but all great beauties lie about their age, and anyway, gods don't have ages or birthdays, even though I had one coming up very soon. The force of him was splitting my brain, not to mention my secret heart, exploding from the light of him—archangel—come to earth, entering my body, possessing me as I breathed, in and out, out and in. God, it was exhausting. So it's no wonder I couldn't understand why my Mummy, and everyone else for that matter, weren't clapping their hands in thunderous applause. Dodo and grandmother Naney Morgan took it hard, as well—Naney Morgan especially, but of course she would. She had been counting on me to catch a personage of royal blood—a prince, a count—a *king* (why not go for that?). Couldn't she see that's what I had? Pat now appeared as some lowly whatever, a munchkin maybe—why not?—now that the Wizard of Oz was by my side.

A few months later, I turned twenty-one. In the never-never land I grew up in at Aunt Gertrude's, there was one and only one F word (as in *forbidden*) and it was *money*. No one talked about money except grown-ups huddled behind closed doors with lawyers. But it was there, always, in back of everything, constantly, continuously, day and night, all the time, nonstop. Neither Aunt Gertrude nor the hated lawyers Gilchrist and Crocker nor anyone else had

ever talked to me about how to manage the inheritance
I was now about to receive. Since I had always felt an
impostor while living with my aunt, the inherited money
seemed unreal, like something that didn't really belong to
me. It was only later that money had reality, because it was
money I earned through my own talent and efforts. The day
I became twenty-one, on the dot, I marched down the long
corridor of Bankers Trust flanked by a parade of bankers,
on down to the vaults where a box was opened. There
inside were the stocks and bonds that would make me an
heiress. I took them out of the box—after all, they were
only paper—what did I know about it? Nothing, that's for
sure. All I knew was that suddenly there was money and
that I couldn't wait to buy presents for everyone: Naney (a
mink coat), Dodo must have one too, diamonds for Carol,
and so on. But Mummy—what to give her? Actually there
was something I wanted *her* to give *me* only I couldn't put
a name to it. Since the allowance Surrogate Foley portioned
out from my trust fund ended now that I had come of age,
Mummy would in the future be depending on me for
support. Tony Furness, Aunt Thelma's millionaire son,
supported his mummy, and I was expected to take care
of mine.

I tried talking to Stokowski about this, but Leopold
was silent, thinking deep thoughts every time I tried. Speak,
speak, talk to me *please*. Days went by, but finally he had it

figured out—"Your mother never gave you love. *Why* give her anything? It was your nanny Dodo who did—your mother never gave you *anything*. Let Thelma support her." Oh—well—maybe—yes—wasn't I in control now? That was a new feeling, strange and liberating—but still . . .

It was no surprise that Mummy didn't take to this one bit. She hotfooted to the press and suddenly there it was, splashed over the tabloids. (How would your mother have viewed this?) They were bing-banging at the door, waiting for us out on the street and every other place you could think of, saying mean, awful things—that Leopold was Svengali and I his Trilby. Can you imagine!? When confronted by reporters, Leopold said, "I never talk about personal things." It was heavy, I can tell you.

It got so freaky that Leopold huddled with his lawyer and came up with the idea of establishing a foundation and then calling a "press conference" to announce it. "Good strategy," the lawyer agreed. Leopold preferred I use the Polish feminine and at the same time change the spelling of my name to Glorya to distinguish me from my mother. It was to be called the Glorya Stokowska and Leopold Stokowski Foundation. I was to be the "secretary" and was photographed behind a typewriter (couldn't type, but so what). Later this photograph appeared in *Time* magazine with a caption under it, "Old Score." What did that mean?

It Seemed Important at the Time

A "press release" was composed stating that my Mummy should find a job and go to work like everyone else did, including me, who was now the secretary of this foundation formed to help those who couldn't work. It was decided that it would be more effective if Leopold wasn't present at the conference. Best if I went to it alone, even without the lawyer. I was told to keep my mouth shut except to say "I never talk about personal things" as I handed out the press release.

Scared to death, I faced the frosty crowd of reporters and got through the ordeal holding fast to the thought that Leopold was waiting for me in another room. It was a terrible feeling, like someone had died—but who? Yes, as if someone had died and I was guilty of killing them and I hated myself because even if the things Leopold said about her were true, she was my mother, the one person in the world I wanted to be mine ever since I could remember. But who could guess that—I didn't even know it yet myself.

After the press conference, I didn't see my mother again for seventeen years.

Gloria Vanderbilt

My Mummy — Later

When I finally saw her again, after seventeen years, she had changed so much I couldn't connect her with the elusive, beautiful woman in the yellow velvet dress I had feared and loved for as long as I could remember. And how I came to see her again had been a long, tortuous route starting with the first words I said to a therapist— "I'm here but I'm never going to talk about my mother." A few years later her name came up, and five years later, after a session with LSD supervised by the same therapist, I finally had the courage to fly out to Los Angeles and knock on the door of the house where she lived with Aunt Thelma on Bedford Drive.

I saw before me a woman so passive, so gentle and tentative it broke my heart, a woman with hysterical blindness, nonetheless real. "Thelma tells me you have a little gray in your hair," she said wistfully. When I left, Wannsie, her devoted maid from that long-ago summer in Hollywood, saw me to the door. "Oh, Miss Gloria," she said, "it was just a misunderstanding." Oh, God help me.

MUCH, MUCH LATER . . .

Today, how I wish my mother was living close by. Perhaps around the corner so that I could drop by for a cup of tea now and then, and tell her about a new love affair, or talk of things that happened long ago but now don't seem as important as they did then. We could smile over the things we may have cried about long ago, as old friends do when they get together once in a while to catch up, to talk about old times and the things that pass.

FANTASIA WITH STOKOWSKI

⟨⟩

Long before I met him, Leopold had built a house in Santa Barbara, California, at the top of a mountain. He called it The Monastery. It was a paradise, and most appropriately named because from the start of our marriage we had lived cloistered, like a sexy monk and nun, scorning what he called Vanity Fair. He had even more or less cut off the relationship with his own daughters, and we never saw them. "Don't let Vanity Fair fool you," he'd warn ominously when later in New York I might venture out on a rare occasion to have lunch with a friend. Well, Thackeray may have had a point: "Ah! Vanitas Vanitatum! Which of us is happy in this world? Which of us has his desire? or, having it, is satisfied?"

Leopold was away now most of the time, conducting in Europe, yes, away more and more, and I no longer traveled with him. I was starting to lose my faith that he was God, but still kept hoping to break through the impenetrable wall he had created around himself.

There were things I wanted to do. I wanted to write. I wanted to paint. I also wanted to be an actress but didn't know yet how to balance the things churning around inside me. He was supportive of my painting, but acting he considered a minor art, and although I sometimes missed not having some sort of life with friends, it had seemed a miracle that Leopold Stokowski, this great musician, the great conductor, a genius, had fallen in love with me, called me his Divine Beloved and had married me. All I'd ever wanted was to please him.

"Oh God, deem me worthy," I'd pray, "deem me worthy of our life together."

But after a while I found myself locked inside a place where I was isolated, suspended in water, water that had frozen. In this ice I couldn't move. Then one day I knew that what I was frozen in was him. And I lost faith. Leopold wasn't God. He wasn't even a false god. He was a fake person, because—I had started to suspect—he was lying to me about himself, and I knew at last that he would never, ever, trust me enough, or allow me to be close to him in the way I longed to be. But how do you tell God that you don't believe in him anymore?

This is how it happened: One evening soon after we were married, he'd crashed into my secret heart, thrilling me with a thunderous moment of intimacy as we sat in front of the fire. There was a mystery in his life no one knew, a secret so secret he'd never told anyone, but he was going to tell me. It had to do with politics and royalty—had I ever wondered why he had a Hapsburg nose? Actually that thought had never occurred to me. What did a Hapsburg nose look like? I couldn't wait to hasten to the library and dig up a portrait, a picture, do intense research—anything to get a grip on what he was talking about. When we first met he had shown me a picture of himself as a baby dressed in frills and lace, but alas, it was all he had left from the family album, which had been stolen. I treasured this picture and

Gloria Vanderbilt

put it in a silver frame next to one of my unknown father. (Later I was to wonder if it really was Leopold or . . . ?) Yes, his family was from Krakow in Poland, and his mother had died soon after he was born, and he was brought up by a beloved nanny who'd been a mother to him very much the way my nanny Dodo had been to me. But now, with this nose revelation—could it be that his father was a prince—a king, even? I'd have to brush up on Austrian history. Maybe he was illegitimate—you know, a love child? Was that the secret? Wow!

As he sat holding my hand, telling me this, the only sound to break the silence was the crackling of the fire, but it was nothing to the crickle-crackling in my heart. It was coming, I could feel it—the moment was rolling in like a gigantic wave about to carry me out into a sea of love. I held my breath, waiting, waiting, but then he took his hand away and looked into the fire as if he was coming out of a trance and the trance was me.

"Yes, yes," he said, "and—someday you will be the only one to know."

But that someday wasn't now, that's for sure. No, the now wasn't going to be then, but it took many winter evenings spent sitting in front of many different fireplaces after many dinners to finally realize that the now wasn't to be—ever, and that I only had a toehold in his heart while he had his whole foot in mine.

IT SEEMED IMPORTANT AT THE TIME

"You're a fake." I trembled as I thought it, but trembled even more later when I looked him in the eye and said it out loud.

Many years after we separated I discovered the secret, but it had nothing to do with a family of Hapsburgs. It had to do with a family of Cockneys that included two brothers, Leopold and Percifal Stokowski. One brother—Leopold—had kept his name, weaving it into a fantasy to suit a great conductor, while Percifal had changed his name to James Stokes to weave around himself the fantasy of an English gentleman. By then Leopold had achieved so much in his long and extraordinary career that he didn't need or care anymore to tend the mysterious facade he had invented about himself. On a trip to Europe he introduced our grown sons to their Uncle Jimmy (Percifal Stokes) and his wife. Jimmy lived in London and had a successful car business selling Rolls-Royces. Younger brother Jimmy had an uncanny resemblance to Leopold save for his Cockney accent, so unlike the Oxford speech Leopold had mastered. Jimmy's son had been named Leopold after Stokowski and had died in the war. And the beloved nanny who had raised Leopold turned out to be his mother, who was living in a nursing home in Bournemouth.

Of course, by the time I found this out his deception didn't matter anymore, and only saddened me. The truth wouldn't have mattered one whit, but he hadn't trusted me enough to know. I would have admired and loved him more (if possible) than I already did—thrilled to have from him the intimacy and trust I craved. What strain and effort must have gone into the constant vigilance required from him all those years to keep up the facade he had created around himself. And when had his imagination taken hold of the idea to reinvent himself? Was it something he and his first wife, Lucie Hickenlooper from the Midwest, had cooked up together when she had reinvented herself as Olga Samaroff and became a concert pianist, while he in turn presented himself as a musician with a mysterious royal past, which to his view had more glamour and prestige than that of a London Cockney?

No, I never did break through to him—except in passion. There he was free and unedited, giving me all of himself in wordless intimacy. But it wasn't enough. Afterward I would be alone once again and living with a stranger, the glass wall impenetrable—"I never speak of personal things." Had I been more mature and less idealistic, what he was able to give me might have been enough and I could have handled it. But his lack of trust in me came as a blow of betrayal—or so I felt at the time. Oh God I did love him so.

No, there was never going to be a key to open the door in that glass wall, leading me to his secret heart. But there was another door next to it, a door leading to a life

It Seemed Important at the Time

without lies, and although I hadn't found the key to it yet, I knew I had to, for if I didn't, I would die.

As I started taking tiny footsteps into what Leopold called Vanity Fair, lo and behold, there waiting on the other side of the glass wall I could see a tiny pied piper. His name was Truman Capote, and he had just appeared on the scene with a book of short stories, *Other Voices, Other Rooms,* told with a literary skill that had captured everyone's imagination. Yes, there he was beckoning with promises of answered prayers. Little did I know then that he of all people certainly didn't have the answer . . . or that no one had the answer but myself.

BREAKFAST AT TIFFANY'S WITH THE TINY TERROR

From the moment I met Leopold Stokowski, all I wanted to do was to please him and make him happy. The summer we were married he was conductor of the Hollywood Bowl orchestra, and I'd sit every day during his rehearsals absorbed and enthralled by his every mood, and though at times I was bored to death at what seemed to me tedious repetition, I never admitted it even to myself. In the years that followed I was to get more than my fill of classical music. So much so that even today I shy away from concerts, and rarely listen to classical music on CDs or the radio. It had also been somewhat of a surprise to discover his suspicious nature and his not wanting some sort of life with family and friends. We had no social life except with each other. But he did support my painting and was enthusiastic in every possible way, and for many years we were happy together. I went on every tour with him throughout the U.S.A. and in Europe, but as the years passed I yearned more and more for home and family, and finally and reluctantly he agreed to an apartment in New York at Ten Gracie Square overlooking the East River. At the same time I rented the top floor of a brownstone, in the Sixties between Fifth and Madison, where I painted.

It was soon after this that Truman Capote and I became friends. I rarely asked anyone to my studio, but Truman had wanted to see it, so one day I invited him there to meet my unexpected houseguest, Russell Hurd. He'd been a friend since childhood, with the looks of Charlton Heston and the wit of Noel Coward. Although Russell was gay, we had been in love with each other ever since the days when we tea-danced at The Plaza. By some fluke, despite being American he had gotten into the Coldstream Guards in England, and much later I found out that he had gone on to be an agent in the CIA. Now he was back in New York at loose ends, not knowing what direction his life was going to take. His trust fund was getting low, so instead of having him stay at a hotel, I asked him to come stay at my studio. What was to be a week turned into months. Russell became the confidant of the new life I was making, and every time the possibility of a love affair for me came into the picture, he would find something to say about the romance (negative, of course). He was so witty we ended up like girlfriends, talking the way they do when there are no men around.

"Where did you find him, honey?" Truman said. No romance, I assured him, but we adore each other.

"So he's living in your studio?"

"Yes, but it's not like it sounds."

"Oh, I know," he said.

But what I didn't know yet was that Truman had started weaving Russell into a story set in a brownstone very like mine, and that the heroine was a girl whose confidant was a man very like Russell. The girl in some

It Seemed Important at the Time

ways was like me, in other ways like Carol Marcus, who was at that very moment on a plane from L.A. to New York, fleeing from her second marriage to the Heathcliffian William Saroyan, with no place to land except at my studio. Russell would have to leave, I told Truman. "What a pity," he said with a sigh.

The relationship I had with Russell continued to intrigue Truman, and for the next few months every time we had lunch he would ask about him. There's no one like Russell, I'd say, but that wasn't what Truman wanted to hear. He really wanted to be the only one to hear the ins and outs of love affairs, especially mine. What he was interested in, and wanted to hear more about, was Russell. More about how I trusted Russell despite his bitchiness, trusted him even to talk to him about Leopold, who in my heart I'd already left, but to whom I was still fiercely loyal. I never discussed Leopold with anyone except Russell. So with Truman I kept up a front, never giving the Tiny Terror a toehold into my oh-so-secret heart. Carol, on the other hand, floored me with her lack of reserve and how open she was about the intimate details, the ups and downs of her life, not just with me and with Truman, but with everyone else. And Truman, sly puss that he was, lapped it up and wove it into *Breakfast at Tiffany's*.

BILL PALEY AND THE TINY TERROR

Truman and I had been friends since our twenties and remained so until he wrote *Answered Prayers,* a book about his friends. I, along with a lot of others, felt betrayed, as well we might. Truman manipulated people, and because he was so intuitive, sensitive, and extraordinary, people trusted him. Many times he tried (sometimes successfully, sometimes not) to manipulate me . . .

Ah, True Heart, as Bill Paley, the president of CBS, used to call him—dear True Heart—I see you sitting over your martini at Pavilion, watching me come toward you quite breathless. I'm late, late, for a very important date, a date with True Heart, who has something up his sleeve, something to talk to me about, something *very* important. That's what he promised on the phone at least.

If you didn't know who he was, you'd have thought I was hastening toward a very much in-charge, self-absorbed slip of a fourteen-year-old schoolboy who detests sports but ends up somehow masterminding the team. He looked much too young to be sipping martinis, his eyes enlarged through the lenses of his glasses, which resembled the bottoms of milk bottles.

I could tell by the look of him, as I settled into the cushy banquette, that he was already on his second martini and that it would be a long lunch with lots of giggles and insights into my secret heart, or so he thought. In truth, he really didn't know that much about my secret heart at all. We were friends, close, but I really never did quite trust him.

Truman always presented himself as an authority. Actually, not just an authority, *the* authority. "I know the way," he once said as we wended our way through a maze of side streets in Greenwich Village, trying to find an obscure restaurant.

"It's this way," I said, pulling him.

"No! No! I know the way," he insisted, as he led me firmly in the opposite direction. He was wrong, of course, but never let on for a second that he didn't know what he was talking about. That was Truman; he drew you into a web, intimating he knew things about you, things you didn't know yourself. How could he betray me when he really didn't know me at all?

But let's get back to lunch, back to what Truman had to say that was so very important.

"Bill Paley." He said the name slowly, his tongue sucking on each syllable. Bill Paley was his close friend, the powerful president of CBS. He was married to the beautiful, kind, loyal Babe. Babe was truly Truman's closest friend. Nevertheless, here Truman was to say that Bill Paley had intimated he was interested in me, and could something be arranged?

"Now wait, honey, just listen to me," Truman said, placing his tiny hand on my arm. "Now, Babe knows that he has other girlfriends and she handles it beautifully, but sometimes it gets out of hand and it gets complicated and messy; it's upsetting to her, naturally. She likes you, you know, respects you; if he was involved with you it would be fun for you, ease things up for her; it would even in a way be doing everyone a favor—so to speak." Truman had a way of presenting things so you'd see them from another point of view. His point of view.

Now, Babe Paley and I were not close friends. I admired her enormously, but was intimidated by how she had edited herself according to her point of view into a mold of perfection and had certainly achieved it in her style, her houses, her garden, her parties, in everything, really. Around her, I never felt I could quite pass muster.

One time we ran into each other at Kenneth's salon, and on the spur of the moment she said, "Are you free for lunch—a sandwich somewhere?" If only that day

Gloria Vanderbilt

I had worn the red Adolfo instead of just a sweater and skirt, I would have said yes. "Oh, how I wish I could, but I've got something," I answered. How ridiculous it seems now; had I responded differently I might have discovered a friend.

"Honey, it's going to take a real pro," Truman said, looking around shiftily. Was I interested? Well—maybe.

IT SEEMED IMPORTANT AT THE TIME

Maybe, I told myself, it would be interesting to get Bill's opinion about a TV show I had recently appeared on. (Oh Gloria, how could you!) And so, a few days later, there I was alone, in Bill Paley's private projection room at CBS, looking at a tape of a television show I had just done with Art Carney called *Very Important People*. Clearly, Bill didn't think what was on the screen was very important at all; he was more captivated by my prim performance leaning away from him.

Truman of course expected a full report on what had transpired. And full report he got. A week later it was another lunch—he had news! Not much, as it turned out. He'd spent the weekend at the Paleys' in Manhasset. Babe had appeared rather testy with Bill (nothing that you could really put your finger on but . . .) and Bill, when they were alone, wanted to know *everything*—what I had said about him and so on. Once again Truman said, "Honey—this is going to take a real pro!"

I did meet Bill alone once again, in his and Babe's place at the St. Regis, a corner apartment that Billy Baldwin decorated with paisley patterns, rich jewel-tone colors, and everywhere objects of ravishing beauty: potpourri in Chinese bowls, sweetpeas in Bristol Blue vases, a Fabergé egg casually left on a table. It was pure unadulterated luxury and I sank into a chair by the fire and thought—why not? He came back from the kitchen with a split of champagne, popping the cork and bounding around like a kid full of plans, talking of places we'd go and things we would do after he got back from the holidays in Jamaica, where he and Babe were going for Christmas. I got up and went over to the window. Looking down on the traffic, the people walking by on Fifth Avenue, I wanted to get out of here and back down there where it was real. No, this just wouldn't do at all. I started to leave and what was to be a calm, sane, civilized farewell turned suddenly into a French farce. I found myself chased, in and out, around the sofa, the chairs, into the bedroom and back again. It really was funny, but at the time it didn't seem so. I just wanted to get the hell out.

Truman called the next day.

"I guess I'm just not a pro," I told him.

"Never mind, honey. How about lunch next Wednesday. There's something else I've got to talk to you about."

DINNER
CHEZ BRANDO

◄══►

I had just seen *On the Waterfront* and flipped over
Marlon Brando. Who hadn't, really? All that inarticulate
sensitivity. So feminine—and yet so masculine. My friend
Russell Hurd and I sat in the darkness of the movie
theater, looking up at the screen, enthralled. Yes, that's
for me, and I couldn't wait to hotfoot it out of the theater
and call Carol on the West Coast. She knew *him,* dated
him even, around New York riding on his motorcycle.
But when I called, her line was constantly busy. Finally
I got through—"Darling, how amazing, I've just been
talking to him on the phone." I'll be right over, I said.
And over I was, on the next plane to L.A.

She picked me up at the airport and we had
dinner at *his* house that very night! Talk about instant
gratification. I had thrown my best Norell dress into the
hastily packed suitcase—red, sari-like, gold-embroidered,
too overdressed for the dinner chez Brando, which turned

out to be a small gathering in the kitchen—Marlon's aunt, Carol, *him,* and me. But no matter: Knees shaking, but outwardly calm, cool, and collected, as they say, I stood outside as Carol rang the doorbell. And there *he* was— more more more everything than even I could have possibly imagined. Of course what I saw really had nothing at all to do with what he was really all about. If Leopold was God, here was Zeus. It took all my concentration not to fall down on the stone pavement in a dead faint.

What did we talk about at dinner? I haven't a clue. The only thing I remember is his saying to me over dessert, over the ice cream and cookies: "You have Japanese skin." Yes, yes, Japanese I wanted to scream— Japanese and it's all for you. But I smiled beguilingly (I hoped) and looked away. Hours trickled by, but then the aunt left, Carol left. I stayed. We were alone at last. Sounds like a romance novel, doesn't it? Guess it was, because once we were alone—oh dear, I don't quite know where I'm taking this now, but anyway—in his bedroom there was a ten-by-twelve drop-dead-gorgeous photograph (himself) in a silver frame on the table by his bed, a glossy studio shot taken to publicize *Désirée,* the movie he was shooting. And next to it a telephone ringing (girlfriends, no doubt), but with the sound switched off so there were only lights twinkling on and off, on and off, all through the night, on and off, glowing like fireflies in the dark.

The next morning Carol came to pick me up. When I got in the car Marlon pressed his lips against the pane of glass on the window between us as I pressed mine in return. But the glass didn't even crack; the only thing cracking was my pitty-pat heart. All day he didn't call. I mooned around Carol's house, waiting for the phone to ring. We talked of nothing else while we made preparations for a party she was giving that night. Should I call him? Should she? No, no, no, definitely not. Wait. He'd show up at the party? Maybe. Would he? No, he wouldn't. Yes, he would. But he didn't. Instead it was Gene Kelly dancing in, singing in the rain of my heart, so to speak, although it perked me up considerably. Once again I was wearing the ill-fated red, sari-like Norell. Gene kept calling me "Persian Princess," and we drifted off into another room and started kissing. During all this Carol and the other guests were horsing around the piano. Betty Comden and Adolph Green were there, and when Gene and I went back to join them, Betty Bacall was singing "Little Girl Blue," describing me perfectly as I looked frantically around. *He* wasn't there. It was getting late and everyone started to leave. I too would be leaving the next day, going back to New York, hollow and empty. Would I ever hear from *him* again?

It turned out to be sooner than I thought—at the airport before boarding the plane. He'd found out my flight from Carol, and there he was on the phone just

before I stepped on the plane. "Thank you for tender feelings," he said. "Me too," I answered casually. But I was in a panic . . . Did you have a premonition that this would turn out as it did?

Back in New York, I not only didn't see him, I didn't hear from him, and I plunged into despair, which I shared with Russell at the studio. We spent hours playing Nat King Cole's record of "Unforgettable." The monotony of it over and over again soothed, comforted me—for God's sake, Gloria, turn it off. Finally Russell had about had it, not only with Nat, but with hearing about Marlon. But I couldn't stop. I was hooked into a myth and couldn't let the tale of enchantment go.

However, despite the fact that my little trip to L.A. wasn't turning out the way I had hoped, it gave me courage. The success I had appearing in my first play, *The Swan*, gave me courage, too. I'd never ever again give myself completely, never again give my secret heart to anyone (even Zeus Marlon) the way I'd given myself to Leopold—no—not in *that* way. From now on I'd give myself only to my work. And by the time Leopold returned from his tour I had worked up enough moxie to ask him once again to let me go. He turned away and didn't even answer, but his silence was a shout of "I'll *never* let you go," which came through his wall of glass bricks loud and clear, and because he was God, I believed him.

THERE'S THAT
PHONE CALL . . .

I'd gotten up the moxie to face Leopold head on, and even though he'd said, "Never never, I'll never let you go," and even though I still somewhere thought maybe he really was God, and even though I was right back in a cage with the door locked, still believing there was no choice but to remain captive, there might be another way to get through to him. Straight to the Scotch bottle I ran, took a couple of swigs to wash down sleeping pills (Seconals, I think), and back I went to where he sat imperiously behind his desk in the library, and I told him that if he didn't let me free, I'd rather die.

Whatever he saw standing in front of him got through to him. It got through and scared him enough to call a doctor, but when the doctor came it wasn't scary enough for me to be sent to the hospital, and still not scary enough for him to let me be free. The only thing free the next day was a hammer bing-banging in my head.

69

Not only had I not gotten through to him—I hadn't gotten through to myself that all I had to do was *go*. Yes—go—*go*, the way I had *go*-ed when I left Aunt Gertrude to be with my Mummy in Hollywood. Go the way I had when I left the Big Bad Wolf to be with Prince-God. It seemed I only had the power to *go* when I had a GREAT THING to go *to*.

Alone with my bing-banging headache, with thoughts like beans jumping around on a hot skittle— what? where? who? how?—and cut off from life, along came one of those phone calls I told you about, the kind that can change your life. Ringie-ding-ding, pick it up on the second ting-a-ling—it's Jule Styne, saying Frank Sinatra was in town and wanted to meet me. Yes! Yes! I jumped out of the frying pan like a squirrel running up a tree, and a week later I took my kids and out we went, out of Ten Gracie Square, out and into the Ambassador Hotel.

 It was so easy. Why hadn't I realized it before? All I had to do was take up my bed and walk, and walk I did. No, not walk, but run—and wild horses couldn't have stopped me.

MIRACLE AND ME

Frank Sinatra exploded into my life like a firecracker.
He had come to New York for a stint at the Copacabana,
a nightclub next to the Hotel Fourteen where my grandmother Naney Morgan lived. I thought of her, sleeping
in troubled dreams only next door, as I sat listening to
Frank's troubling songs: "It's a quarter to three, there's
no one in the place except you and me." For one crazy
moment I thought of running to her . . . but would she
hear me if I knocked on her door?

Having made a great comeback success in the
movie *From Here to Eternity*, Sinatra had also just separated
from his wife, actress Ava Gardner, and was hot-hot again,
right up there with the shooting stars, and he was taking
me right up there with him. Right behind us followed the
tabloid press—it was quite a scandal. But I didn't care a
fig. Even if I had seen the trashy headlines, it wouldn't have
made any difference. Ever since the publicity I'd had as
a child, I rarely read anything written about myself in
newspapers, and this was certainly not the time to start.

IT SEEMED IMPORTANT AT THE TIME

I wanted to stay *clear,* keep focused on the things I wanted to do, and although reading about myself in newspapers wouldn't have turned me into a pillar of salt, it might momentarily make me question the creation—the invention, you might say—of what I aspired to.

Even the excellent reviews I'd received for my debut in the play *The Swan,* which producer Gilbert Miller had sponsored for a tryout in Rowena Stevens's theater in Pennsylvania, had gone unread, but I knew the play was a hit because all the agents were after me. And I, knowing nothing about the theater, signed with the most persistent—unfortunately, for she hadn't seen me in the play, and kept telling me not to listen to Gilbert Miller, who wanted to bring the play to Broadway. "You don't want to be that silly princess," she reasoned, "you want to be the girl next door." Did I? Was I? The girl next door? Obviously she wanted to be in control, forceful in her attitude, and because I thought she knew more about the theater than I did, unfortunately I listened to her. Later, Sidney Lumet told me that actors long for a vehicle, and I knew that I'd made a big mistake in turning down Gilbert Miller. Instead the agent placed me in a minor part in Saroyan's *The Time of Your Life.* Carol Marcus, then still in her second marriage to Saroyan and also embarking on an acting career, was playing an important role. Saroyan was coaching her.

But when I made my flight from Ten Gracie Square we hadn't started rehearsals yet, and as I got to know Frank Sinatra, I came to see him in a very different way from the many varied images of him floating around. Harold Arlen, smitten and protective of me, and fearing I might be hurt, told Frank, "Herm, be nice to tender people" (they always called each other "Herm"). And indeed Herm was—not only nice, but tender and sweet, showering me with attention, romantic attention, and plans for the future. Plans to go to Bali together, dreams of love, but even better, dreams of working together in the movies, and—best present of all—signing me to a contract with his production company for a three-picture deal, one to be *Ocean's Eleven*. There were midnight suppers during which he talked about himself, confiding the split in his mind, like a balance scale, on one side

It Seemed Important at the Time

Mafia-dark, on the other side Clark Kent–light, dark and light, up and down, a pull drawing him to the dark, but in the end Clark always triumphed.

Yes, he loved to talk about himself (most men do); I, on the other hand, hadn't been able to get a word in edgewise, and I was eager to confide in him my enthusiasm for Albert Schweitzer, who preoccupied me much of late. Best give him the book I was reading, which defined Schweitzer's philosophy of "reverence for life," including all living things, even bugs—yes, bugs. What would Frank have to say about that? But he didn't seem all that interested, so I let it drop.

We often double-dated with actress Joan Blondell and sports columnist Jimmy Cannon. Frank and Jimmy talked about Frank, while Joan and I listened and smiled a lot. We went to the opening of the musical *Pajama Game,* mobbed by the paparazzi, but I didn't care. I was free, alive again. At his Copa opening I was thrilled when he caught my eye while singing "A Foggy Day in London Town"—just for me.

And although he drank Jack Daniel's, I never saw him drink too much or be rude or violent to anyone, as some well-intentioned friends kept warning me about. There were presents, too. A gold bracelet with a dangling charm "From miracle and me" in diamonds. And that's just how it was—a miracle coming at exactly the right

moment, for hadn't he
rescue me by giving
me the power to leave
Leopold? I couldn't have
done it without him.

But why? Why
did I need someone to
rescue me, when all I had
to do was rescue myself?
Somehow I was back
where I'd been as a child,
feeling I had no control over my life. Somehow I was still
there, desperately looking around, here, there, everywhere,
seeking somebody to show me the way. But there was
nobody home. Aunts, mothers, grandmothers, along with
bank presidents, doctors, lawyers—they were in AUTHORITY.
They were in control, in power.

They knew something about me I didn't know
myself, but they wouldn't tell me what it was. You know,
Kafkaesque.

And even now, much later, somewhere there
were Higher-Ups lurking around in control—*Authorities*
in charge. I had the power to move only when a more
powerful Authority than the one in charge came along to
back me up. I left Aunt Gertrude only after I thought I'd
met my Mummy, left Pat only after I met Stokowski, left

him only when Frank came along. Why couldn't I have left because I'd met myself?

Yes, Sinatra ringie-dinged his way, circling around my secret heart, but I didn't let him into the center, to the bull's-eye, so even though he was about to leave town, ringie-dinging off on a tour in Australia, I wasn't too upset. Soon I'd be ringie-dinging out to L.A. to star in a movie with him, but until then there were lots of others ready to ringie-ding with me right here in little old New York. There was mad, bad, and dangerous-to-know Lawrence Tierney, who was also one of the many actors cast in the Saroyan play as we started rehearsals. He'd had a huge success in his first movie, *Dillinger*, playing the gangster, but had sabotaged his career by erratic exploits, and now despite this was being given another chance by our producer, Jean Dalrymple. Images shot into my mind's eye the moment we met—eyes like steel found me, made me sense that I could be the stream to feed the roots, for his love seemed like a tree, needing a strange alchemy from my eyes—green moss, absorbing his eyes that shut me out. How about them apples? All he needed was me to ease his dark-blue pain. But was it dark blue? Or simply dark gobbledy-gook?

There were rumors of drunken rages, walking into Catholic churches naked during High Mass. Surely not? Surely it was only gossip from those jealous of his gorgeous good looks and sensitive talent. Do you think you're a keener judge of character now than you were ten years ago?

He scribbled poetry to me on paper napkins in coffeehouses as we sat philosophizing about this and that—obscure bits and pieces, passed wordlessly across the table like furtive notes in school, strange and brilliant but making no sense. But what is "sense" coming from a poet, inarticulate and shut off from everyone save the few such as *moi* who had the sensitivity to understand him.

He wasn't drinking (or was he?), but one day in rehearsal he made a scene as if he was, and our director, Sandy Meisner, fired him. It made him more fascinating than ever. But the situation was getting more and more out of hand, you know—complicated. The play opened, and one night he appeared at the theater after a performance, not dark blue but a disturbing shade of wicky-wacky dark red. Nothing soothed him; little did I know how wicky-wacky *that* possibility was.

Then the next day, just before I was to make my entrance on national live TV to do a brief scene with Franchot Tone on the *Colgate Comedy Hour,* a phone call came from Larry. He sounded ill, in dire need—rattled, off balance.

Now rattled too, I went on the air, blew my lines—not only blew them, they went completely out of my head. It was very, very important at the time—it was like the earth caving in or like being hit by a ton of bricks or Vesuvius erupting—yes, more like that—definitely.

My contract to star in a Jack Webb movie was canceled, and then it was blackout doomsday. Or so it seemed. I knew it was me who was wicky-wacky. I wasn't meant to be Florence Nightingale after all, nor did I want to be . . . or did I? But no matter. Tierney had unsettled me, nothing more. Soon after I was on my feet again, up-and-at-'em. My secret heart untouched, still intact. But it was never in danger—after Leopold no one was ever going to find it again.

And what did Lawrence Tierney find? Unfortunately more of the same. I suspect he always found one Florence Nightingale or another who felt she was the one to save him, but his career foundered—and he got odd jobs here and there. I heard he'd taken a job driving one of those hansom cabs that wait around The Plaza hotel in New York. But I did see him once again years later on Broadway as I came out of a theater. He was almost unrecognizable slumped against a parked car in no condition to catch my eye. My impulse was to go to him. But I didn't. I walked on by. I knew there was nothing I could do to save him.

KING ARTHUR AND LADY GUINEVERE

◄——►

If Franchot Tone was King Arthur searching (as he told me) for Lady Guinevere, then who better than me to step into that part?

As a child, I first saw him on a silver screen in a dark theater. Gazing up at the scenes, I strained to get a hint of what it was going to be like when I grew up. Then *I* would be in control, not controlled by the grown-ups around me. I couldn't wait. How handsome, how debonair Franchot Tone was, and hadn't he been married to Joan Crawford? Romanced Bette Davis? Wow! He also had been part of the Group Theatre—impressive! Serious, you know.

But now here I was, grown up (or a reasonable facsimile). Not only grown up, but acting in a William Saroyan play with him. Co-starring, so to speak. And he was attracted to me, although I wondered which *me* it was. When it came right down to it, I didn't know which one myself. We spent a lot of time at Birdland and other

hot spots, and he sent flowers with notes saying things like "I love you in the many mirrors of the real, but really too." I thought about that. How many times a day do *you* look at yourself in the mirror? There was a gentleness about him, a fineness, but by the end of an evening he would descend fuzzily into a passive melancholy that reminded me of the Clifford Odets play *Golden Boy*. "I have a lump inside and I drink to dissolve it." But it was too late for that and I wasn't the drink he was looking for. Soon after, Sinatra winged along and we parted without even saying good-bye. All along we'd both known that whatever we had together was transient, but isn't everything, really? It's only when you expect permanence that life disappoints you.

A Red Rose

Sinatra had ringie-dinged away on his tours, attentively calling from Australia, Hawaii, Las Vegas, wherever. He was on my mind, but not as much as the professional acting classes I had begun taking under Sanford Meisner at the Neighborhood Playhouse. That was what was *really* on my mind. Carol Marcus Saroyan was still staying at my studio, and she also enrolled in the class. And she had a new name, christened by the Heathcliffian Saroyan: Carol Grace. "You'll be like an ocean liner—you know, the Grace Line, toot-tooting out to sea," he said, not without a tinge of undisguised hostility.

We were a dedicated group in Sandy's class— George Peppard, Suzanne Pleshette, Steve McQueen, Peter Falk, Marti Stevens, Pat Boone, Joanne Woodward, Anita Ellis, Timmy Everett, Sidney Pollock, and so on. All we thought about were our careers.

As for me, I *never* wanted to get married again— never again give my secret heart to anyone the way I had to Leopold. From now on I'd go my way by myself—

81

whoever *myself* was. Although I had moved out of Ten Gracie Square and was staying in a hotel, Leopold refused to leave. He *knew* I'd be back.

Richard Avedon photographed me for *Harper's Bazaar,* and he was saying, "There's someone I'd like you to meet: Sidney Lumet, a director. He's just separated from his actress wife, Rita Gam. I think you'd each have something to give the other." I was intrigued—a director— maybe we would work together (Garbo and Stiller?). Fun to dream, isn't it? Why not?

A week later the Avedons gave a dance at their house on Beekman Place for Grace Kelly. I had little sleeveless short dresses made of satin in an array of delicious colors, long-waisted, in an F. Scott Fitzgerald mode, with pumps dyed to match, and that night I picked the framboise to wear. I fluffed up my hair and out I went alone to the party. And there he was, waiting for me— Sidney Lumet, enfolding me in his arms like a teddy bear. As we danced I could feel the energy of his heart and soul going through me like warm honey. How's that for romance? But then I got panicky because he said he had to leave the party to meet an agent at Sardi's.

I didn't think he'd come back. "Bet a red rose you won't," I told him. I was sure there would be some glamour girl with the agent, and he'd forget all about me. But he did come back; he did; he not only came back, he

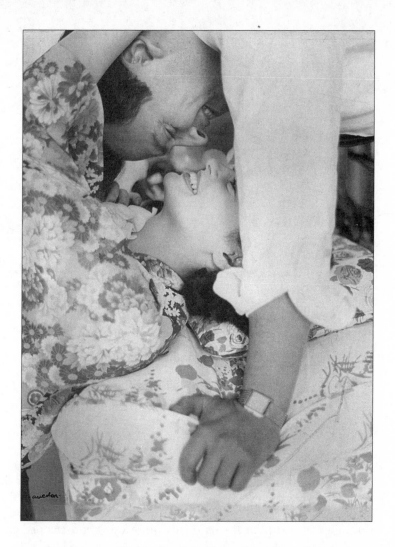

was holding a red rose (exactly the color of my framboise dress), and together we left the party, and from that moment on we were glued each to the other—so glued that our friends found it hard to be around us. But that was OK, because all we wanted was to be alone together.

OF PINK TONGUES AND HOW SERIOUS AND SINCERE IT ALL WAS

Sidney didn't want to be in love ever again with an actress, and he knew I was dead set on being just that. But when I left for L.A. to do the movie with Sinatra and he saw me off at the airport, he knew it didn't matter because by then I was totally in love and committed to him. He could see that.

Exhausted from so much love, I fell asleep on the plane. When I awoke, seated beside me wasn't the stranger who was there when we took off, but instead, through some kind of hocus-pocus there was another one there. John Huston introduced himself. He was utterly charming throughout the trip, but I was mesmerized by his tongue. It was so—so pink—pink as a Popsicle, and I couldn't stop looking at it.

Later, back in New York relating my adventures in

Gloria Vanderbilt

wonderland to our Tiny Terror: "His tongue. I've never considered a tongue as a feature of the face, but I couldn't stop looking—it was so so pink!"

"Honey," Truman said, "that's because it's had a lot of practice!" So much for pink tongues.

Frank was to have met me at the airport but unexpectedly chose not to (miffed about Sidney?). His car was there, however, and when I got to my bungalow at the Beverly Hills Hotel there were flowers, champagne, and a message from him in Palm Springs.

We were scheduled to star together in *Johnny Concho,* but I was dismayed as I settled in to read the script and found a trashy Western, not in the same serious league of *High Noon* as I had been led to believe. Frank blamed it all on the director Don Maguire, saying, "I'll deal with him in my own way." (Oh dear.)

I couldn't wait to call Sidney and tell him I was on my way back home to him. But was I? What I was really going back to was my intense preoccupation with studying acting at the Neighborhood Playhouse. Yes, moment to moment, how serious and sincere it was. Let me tell you the things I loved about acting. I loved starting the rehearsal of a play, the feeling of belonging to what I imagined a family to be like (temporary though it was), knowing that as in a family there would be altercations, fights, romance (I always got a crush on my leading man),

but nevertheless we'd hang in, sticking together at least until after the play closed and the "family" broke up. But after that there'd be another opening, another show, and with it another family (even if between jobs I agonized that I would never find one again).

The ritual of blocking a play—I loved that, it gave me something to depend on. However, I was temperamentally totally unsuited to being an actress. By nature I work best alone, within the solitary demands of writing and painting, not having to depend on a script, director, other actors, anyone except myself. My obsession, commitment, and determination to be an actress had a lot, an awful lot, to do with wanting to impress my Mummy, to get her attention. After opening night of my first play I asked Russell Hurd, Did I look thin on stage? (Thinness was much admired by Mummy.) "Yes, darling," he assured me. No, no, tell me, did I look *really* thin? "Yes, yes, you couldn't have looked thinner." Out of pain, I cried angrily, "That'll show the bitch"—as if I had achieved something. But what? (How pathetic.) She lived in Europe and probably didn't even know I was in a play, much less pursuing an acting career.

Soon after this in a *Look* magazine article producer Gilbert Miller, who had launched me in *The Swan* and had been presenting London and Broadway hits for thirty-nine years, was quoted, "I can count the stars I have discovered on the fingers of one hand. There was Ruth Chatterton, Leslie Howard, Audrey Hepburn, and now Gloria Vanderbilt. She needs training, Lord knows she needs training, but she has a running head start in theater—an electric presence, dignity, poise, intelligence, beautiful speech. Her maternal grandmother is Chilean; maybe she inherits that Latin creativity." But I knew in my secret heart no matter how famous I ever became, no matter how great a success I was as an actress, it would *never* be enough. Even if, through luck and perseverance, I could have turned my tiny talent into a combination of Duse, Bernhardt, and Laurette Taylor, it would never have gotten "anywhere near where the trouble is," as Miss Adelaide sings in *Guys and Dolls.*

Sidney did everything he could to support and further my career, but it was never enough, and soon it brought out things in me I didn't like. It was also subtly seeping into our relationship. Judy Holliday, the great comedienne, told me she regarded acting as a "disease." I knew exactly what she meant. Some can handle it, of course, but though I gave it all I had for seven years, I hated almost every minute of it.

FORTUNE COOKIES

Sidney Lumet was born into the theater, and when I met him he was a director whose star was soaring in what was later called "The Golden Age of Television." His father, Baruch Lumet, had been prominent in the Yiddish theater. Sidney became a child actor, performing in Sidney Kingsley's *Dead End,* and later, as a teenager he starred as the young Jesus in *The Eternal Road,* directed by Max Reinhart. We got a smile out of Brooks Atkinson's review in *The New York Times* describing Sidney's Jesus costume "as something out of the Junior Miss department at Saks Fifth Avenue." One night after the performance he listened through the partition between dressing rooms and heard Arlene Francis, who played Mother Mary, chatting with a friend. "Any horny guys in the cast?" he heard the friend ask Arlene. "No, not really, except for Sidney." "Oh?" "Yes, every night when we do that scene as I kneel down and draw him to me—he gets a hard-on." "No kidding, how old is he?" "Twelve," Arlene answered, "a little *too* young for me."

Actually he wasn't; he had knocked a few years off his age to get the part. After Pearl Harbor and the Signal Corps, he started working in television, directing the series *You Are There,* a remarkable anticipation of our live reportage ahead. When we met he was directing the live shows *Studio One* and *Elgin Specials,* and was about to direct his first movie, *Twelve Angry Men,* which turned out to be one of the great films of the year and now is considered a classic.

Being born in the same year was one of the magical things we shared—like those songs to which I knew all the lyrics. He loved to hear me sing in my wavery voice as we drove in his MG around "Manhattan, the Bronx, and Staten Island too—Mott Street too was lovely in July and so was going through the zoo." We'd have long Sundays together, a breakfast of French toast, listening to Jo Stafford, and then maybe we'd go to

Pearl's Chinese restaurant for supper. The first time we went there, we opened our fortune cookies; his read, "Rise, take up thy bed and walk" (he had just separated from Rita Gam), and mine, "You have met love and all is well" (what signs and portents of the feelings exploding inside us).

He was the warmest, most loving person, the most open, unedited person I had ever met. So why did we part? What happened to our great love? Maybe getting married. Although I loved him, I still didn't want to be married. I didn't want more children yet—he did, of course. I kept putting it off—someday when I've achieved more. And that someday kept being pushed further and further ahead.

Everything I wanted seemed waiting just around the corner. But was it? What I really wanted wasn't just around the corner, it was right there with Sidney, only I didn't have the confidence in myself to see it. He gave all of himself and often would say, "You're not giving *all* of yourself." "I am, I am!" I'd cry. But maybe he was right. My secret heart was locked away so it could never be hurt again. We're back now to romance novels, right? But how else to put it?

Over the Rainbow at Ten Gracie Square

When Sidney and I married, a friend of his father, stunned, said, "The son of Baruch Lumet married a shiksa?!" Shiksa though I may be, he was crazy in love with me and I with him. Leopold had accepted the fact that I wasn't going back to him. Finally he had moved out and we divorced. Together Sidney and I made the penthouse at Ten Gracie come alive again. Here legendary parties flourished. When Jule Styne arrived at our parties he would always head straight to the piano to play the songs he had composed over the years. It would be Judy Holliday beside him, or Lisa Kirk, or Marilyn Monroe singing as she tried to remember the lyrics to "Diamonds Are a Girl's Best Friend." Lena Horne with Harold Arlen at the piano playing his "Over the Rainbow," Adolph Green singing Captain Hook songs from his musical *Peter Pan*, or he and Betty Comden singing "Just in Time" from

Bells Are Ringing along with Judy Holliday, while Truman Capote spooked around for something to write about.

At one of my birthday parties Steve Sondheim for the first time sang the lyrics of *Gypsy,* which hadn't gone into rehearsal yet, while Jule accompanied him on the piano. We gave another party for Truman, to say bon voyage to the Tiny Terror before he headed to Russia to write *The Muses Are Heard.* This was a report about the American production of *Porgy and Bess* that traveled by train from East Berlin to Leningrad in the U.S.S.R., where the opera

was to have its Russian premiere, an event destined to gain worldwide attention.

Then there was the party for Isak Dinesen, in New York to lecture on her book *Out of Africa.* She came escorted by Carl Van Vechten, who had become a close friend. We ensconced her in a throne (so to speak) in our library, with a little table by her side so she could reach from time to time for the green seedless grapes, oysters on a bed of ice in a golden bowl, and champagne, for she ate nothing else. She sat like a fragile, thin black spider, as guests came to pay homage. She adored Sidney, who carried her out to our terrace with its view of the nighttime skyline and the lights of the city reflected in the river far below.

Marilyn Monroe, who had fled to New York from Hollywood to form her own production company with Milton Green, came to our parties unrecognizable, wearing a baggy army/navy sweater, slacks, and no makeup save a bit of Vaseline on her eyelids. We huddled together one night, separated from the party while she talked about Joe DiMaggio—how she had been afraid of him although she didn't know quite why. But I did—both of us were fatherless; therefore, we believed all things possible and nothing safe.

There were these parties, and parties we went to, and openings of plays, but most of all, there was work. Whenever the opportunity came, Sidney and I worked, whether together or separately, and still I kept putting off having children—that was for later. But the only "later" for Sidney and me came much, much later . . .

I'm writing about the search for love, not about love found—that's another story. With Wyatt Cooper I not only found love, I found for the first time the happiness of a secure, stable family life. When you love someone, it is *inconceivable* that that person is going to die—at least that is how it was for me. But Wyatt did die—a heart attack. He was only fifty. Our son Carter was twelve and Anderson ten. For a long time I was in denial—he was on a trip and would come back. But he didn't. The man who came back into my life was Sidney Lumet. He had just separated from Gail Jones (Lena Horne's daughter), having married her after he and I parted. He had two daughters with Gail, and although Sidney and I hadn't seen each other during our subsequent marriages, it seemed inevitable that we'd meet again. And meet again we did. When Sidney and I had separated he left his wedding ring in the drawer of the night table by our bed. I kept it along with mine in a velvet-lined silver box my grandmother Morgan had given me. The rings had a history. Sidney had

bought them at Cartier a
month after we met, even
though he was still married
to Rita Gam and I to
Leopold. They had waited
in the familiar Cartier paper
in two red leather gold-
embossed boxes—a promise
for our future. Inside his
was inscribed Gloria, and
inside mine, Sidney. When
we met again so many years
later I asked him what he
had done with his Gloria
wedding ring. Threw it in
the East River, he said. No,

darling, I told him, I have it. He had no recollection of
having left it in the drawer. Immediately he was talking
of marriage (Would you do it over again?), even though
he wasn't divorced yet from Gail. With loving enthusiasm
he moved ahead fast, making plans to enlarge his house
on 91st Street so that my boys and I could move in. There
was love between us—there always will be, but everything
was moving much too fast.

When summer came, we sped back and forth
between our houses in East Hampton and Southampton.

IT SEEMED IMPORTANT AT THE TIME

Sidney couldn't be alone (most men can't), and he kept pressing forward, until one weekend in East Hampton, Neil Simon and Marsha Mason were coming to his house for dinner, and sitting in the garden before they arrived Sidney started talking about "Doc" (Neil Simon) and his marriage to Marsha, which had taken place a few weeks after the death of Simon's first wife. I can't understand that, I said. How could he remarry so soon after? "Let the dead be dead," he answered. The words stunned me . . . It really got to me, and later I told him it would be best if we didn't see each other for a while. Maybe I was right, he said. He had never been alone and perhaps it *was* a good idea to spend time alone in East Hampton to see what it was like. Not for long, as it turned out, for he started seeing more and more of Mary Bailey Gimble, who lived near him in the country, and soon after they were married.

From time to time I see them from a distance, usually at a party across a crowded room, and it makes me happy to know he's found the perfect person at last. He deserves the best.

LE DIVORCE

<small>⬦</small>

How do you feel about divorce? It happens a lot in our country, but in Europe less so because the pursuit of romantic love is perceived differently; in some countries divorce doesn't exist at all. Here divorce is often referred to as a "failed marriage." I don't see it that way. To me a "failed marriage" would be to accept a loveless marriage. But let's face it—love can be complicated, and if it leads not to heaven, it may lead to le divorce. And that *is* hell. I've been divorced twice. I don't count le divorce from Pasquale De Cicco, because I don't consider it was a marriage and could have had it annulled, had I not been so impatient to marry Leopold. Yes, there's no getting around it, divorce is hell, and when you have children it's even more hell.

My divorce from Sidney Lumet was hell because he had been not only a wonderful husband and stepfather to my two Stokowski sons, but at times I hadn't been fair to him and sometimes behaved badly. But my divorce from Leopold was double-trouble hell because he was the father

of my children. He proposed that I continue on in our marriage "with or without," but that would never have been acceptable and after long, drawn-out, painful negotiations he finally did agree to a divorce and I was free.

So what can I say to you about divorce? Try not to think of it as "failure." There were times when it wasn't failing; there were times when it was glowing and glorious. Put on a scale, they might even outweigh the hell part. And if they don't—press on. Without black there can't be white. Good and bad, white = good, black = dark; there would be no white = good if we didn't have black = bad to compare it with. It's a Zen teaching worth contemplating. And while you're at it, contemplate yourself and what got you wanting to divorce in the first place. Maybe give the idea of le divorce a rest for a while, stop thinking about it, and when you do shake the dice around a bit, do another throw. The numbers will roll out differently and you'll see things in a new way. Maybe. Maybe not. Then breathe in and out, out and in. Bring some yoga into the picture. Ease up on yourself—and him or her. If I had done that I might never have divorced Leopold. Or Sidney. But then think what I would have missed—Wyatt and the family I'd longed for with the birth of our beloved sons, Carter and Anderson. See what I mean? As D. H. Lawrence wrote at the very end of *Lady Chatterly's Lover,* "The future is still to hand." Think about it.

ONCE THERE WAS A COUPLE . . .

Someday I'll write a memoir about family happiness, but this isn't the place for it. But I mention it now so you know my restless search for love didn't remain unanswered.

One evening at a dinner party in New York I met Wyatt Cooper, whose eyes were the bluest I'd ever seen, and when they met mine there was the shock of recognition between us and we fell in love. Wyatt was a writer born in Quitman, Mississippi, and later when I met his large, loving family, I was overwhelmed to see what it must have been like to experience a supportive family behind you. I knew then that I wanted him to be the father of my children. Yes, we both wanted the same thing—to start our own family. And what an extraordinary father he was. He was the most honest person I've ever met and his sense of values taught me what the loving parenting I never had could be like.

Gloria Vanderbilt

The dedication of Wyatt's book *Families: A Memoir and a Celebration,* published by Harper & Row, is "To my two families, the one that made me and the one I made." I reread his memoir often, and although death intervened and took him from us, the memory of the life we created together with our two sons, Carter and Anderson, lives on in my secret heart, nourishing and sustaining me through the days of my life.

Gloria Vanderbilt

ROCK BOTTOM

My twenty-three-year-old son Carter had been
taking a nap on our living room sofa on a staggeringly
hot afternoon in July. Suddenly he came into my bedroom
dazed, saying, "What's going on? What's going on?" Then
he turned suddenly and ran, fast, fast through the hall and
up the stairs onto the terrace of our building. I ran after
him, calling out—"Carter! Carter!"—but he didn't hear me.

There isn't a day that I don't think of him, and
once again go over and over the events that followed as
I stood there facing him on the terrace of our thirteenth-
floor apartment as he took his own life (it happened in
seconds). Suicide has always been a word surrounded
with such stigma . . . such terrible dread. Breaking that
stigma, talking about it is important, as important as it
is to talk about all tragedies that befall us. No one who
knew Carter understood why it happened then, and
fifteen years later we still do not understand. Why?

Closure and *survivor* are words we hear all the
time these days. "You need to find closure," a well-

meaning friend said to me after Carter's death. There is, of course, no such thing as closure—ever. And there shouldn't be. Faulkner said, "The past is never dead— it's not even past." And *survivor*? I've never been entirely comfortable with that term either, although I haven't yet found a substitute for it.

It is completely understandable to cry out—Why *me*? But why *not* me? Why is *me* exempt, because if we live long enough, sooner or later all of us come to our own tragedies—our own rock bottoms. Few escape. When it happens—the unthinkable—all that is left is choice. You choose whether or not to keep on living . . . You choose whether or not to survive.

After Carter's death, there were moments when I didn't want to go on living. It was like being buried under rocks, under the sea, only I was left with the ability to breathe, left with the torture of being alive. His death happened in seconds, and in a blink—knowledge of beauty, intuition, logic, space, time—all I had known of reality was forever altered.

It's the random things one remembers, images and flashes—like one friend, a powerful force in the publishing field, walking into my house after the funeral, and when I saw him I thought, He's a messenger, the authority come to tell me that it hadn't happened, that Carter wasn't dead. That it was all some kind of terrible joke. Haven't you had these moments that dart into your mind from out of nowhere, unrelated to reality and yet not so, because they give us a moment's respite from pain?

Those we love are part of us in death, alive in our memory as they were in life. I am as close to Carter now as I was then. Seen from the back, someone in a crowd

looks so like him I almost run to catch up. I hear his laughter and see his smile. And the sorrow, despite the passing of time, doesn't diminish, it just changes.

Do anything that helps you to live one moment through to the next. It helped me a great deal to join a support group. I entered the room a stranger, but later, sitting in a circle, talking or simply listening, no one was a stranger to another. More than friends, we were a family, for pain strips you bare. We knew each other well.

After our meetings I'd walk home through the park and find myself stopping beneath a tree and circling the trunk with my arms, letting myself go, feeling my spirit flowing up to the branches, on up to the sky above. In the street, I felt wordless communication with strangers passing. People at outdoor cafés, a woman walking her dog—they weren't alien to me. I knew their pain, their joy—yes, even remembered joy—for although reeling in a dimension where even the memory of joy seemed forever lost, I knew that for others it existed somewhere. I too had had it in my life. No one would ever be a stranger to me again, because I knew that if it hadn't come already, the day *would* come when they too would have to live through tragedy and loss as we all do, and this connects us now and forever. By giving myself to the visceral pain, not fighting it, I gained strength as each moment passed, a strength I hadn't had the moment before. And with it came the overpowering will to survive, and in doing so to quicken the vibrations of the whole earth.

I got through each day moment to moment. I worked then, as I work now, to *stay clear*—knowing that the anguish, despite passing of time, never goes away, but learning to live with it, one moment to the next, forming an image of myself as a sieve, letting the pain pass through me to become a mantra, a meditation— STAY CLEAR STAY CLEAR—the grief passing through, water through a sieve so that it wouldn't lodge inside to clog and fester, turning me into something I didn't want to become.

In my mind's eye I see everyone in the world as links in an endless chain, including you and me, connected by an energy of compassion. So let's be kind to each other, for everyone we meet is fighting a great battle.

We are all part of the mysterious, unknown energy, part of the never-ending cycle of life and death. In the words of the fourteenth-century mystic Julian of Norwich, which I *sometimes* believe, "Love is not changed by death and nothing is lost and all in the end is harvest." It sounds pretty important, yes, but we all have to try to figure it out for ourselves. We all have to believe in something.

THE FANTAST

───

I've been involved with three married men in my life. Take it from me, if you are even vaguely tempted—don't! Roald Dahl was the first and meant nothing to me, and if he hadn't become such a successful writer he would have faded into the landscape. He was rather like a very dry lemon, but for some reason I still have his letters, as well as a handwritten manuscript of a short story he gave me as a present. It's in a file somewhere, and someday I'll send them to his second wife for his archives. I'll tell you about it later if you're interested. Bill Paley was the second. Let's call them the Minors, because the third was the Major. Yes, definitely. I'll call him the Major, because his wife is still around and it wouldn't be fair—she'll know, I suppose, but really she always has. We were involved, if that is the word, for fifteen years in the sorry tale I'm about to tell.

I met the Major, who is a photojournalist, on a shoot when my first memoir, *Once Upon a Time,* was published by Knopf. I had been on a long tour and was

───
Gloria Vanderbilt

on the last lap when I agreed to be photographed for *People* magazine. But since I didn't want them taking pictures in my house, it was arranged that the shoot would take place in Knopf's offices. For some silly reason I remember what I wore—a creamy cashmere sweater with a long black-and-white zig-zaggy print silk skirt. I remember also that I was bone tired and in no mood to be photographed.

In one of the rooms a table had been set up with a vase of white peonies, placed next to a Queen Anne wing chair in front of a wall of books. When I got to the windowless room the door was open. It was dark inside save for a spotlight on the chair. There appeared to be no one in the room. I sat down, and after a moment, a figure stepped out from the darkness and introduced himself. There was something theatrical about it—like an actor making an entrance onstage—yet at the same time it was silent and simple. It was as if something had fallen into place.

Later I went to speak at a book lunch, and he showed up unexpectedly, taking more pictures. I remember there was a turquoise-emerald silk handkerchief in his breast pocket (I learned he had dozens of the same and almost always wore one for luck). There was about him an irresistibly appealing quality—like an athletic physique in which masculine strength is given a slight touch of feminine grace. He also had an unending supply of charm, of which I was a principal recipient in the years to come.

IT SEEMED IMPORTANT AT THE TIME

As I was leaving the luncheon, he asked me to sign my book, and said he'd like to shoot more photographs. I was going the next day to Boston for an appearance, leaving very early in the morning. "I'll be there at seven," he said: "We can shoot before you leave."

The next morning there he was, sitting in the lobby of my apartment building, camera at the ready. We went into the nearby park, where he clicked away, charming as all get-out. I knew he was smitten (you can always tell), and no doubt he knew it was mutual. He didn't wear a wedding ring, and he certainly wasn't acting like the very, very married man that I came, as the years passed, to realize he was.

At our first lunch he asked me to go to Tunisia with him on a shoot. I almost accepted. Not that day, but soon after, in fact, he told me he was "getting a divorce." He said his longtime wife was also his secretary and went on to say she was "not a bad person, but she embarrasses me," and so on . . .

Oh dear—from the beginning I believed every word. And so began the seesaw days, up and down, the highs, the lows. The pitter-pat, the weak-in-the-knees, the waiting for the phone to ring.

The wife—a whirligig set into orbit—called me, screaming, "Leave him alone."

"Don't talk to *me* about this—talk to *him*," I calmly told her. But I was shaking as I hung up.

All day she kept calling. I finally took the phone off the hook, telling the doorman in my building not to let her up since I thought she might whirl over like a banshee to confront me. (Sounds like something out of *Cosmo*, doesn't it?)

Then something unthinkable happened. My beloved son Carter took his own life. I was there when it

IT SEEMED IMPORTANT AT THE TIME

happened. I had a date to meet the Major that night for dinner. We were to meet at San Domenico at seven-thirty. He knows I'm never late. When I didn't show up, he called to find out why. "Do you want me to come?" he said. Yes, I told him. Yes. But he didn't. He didn't come. What happened the rest of that terrible night I've already told you about, and this is the night that he failed me when I needed him most. I realized he had no guts, no courage to stand by me, the person he professed to love. I never wanted to see him again. Ever.

In the days that followed, with the determination of a Rottweiler he bombarded my house with phone calls. If I didn't hang up on him, anyone who answered the phone hung up on him, but on and on it went. He wouldn't stop.

As the weeks went by, mail kept piling up—from friends, strangers, people sending sympathy and support. My friend Ben Brantley would come over to help me go through the accumulated mail. I'd lie on the bed as he sat in front of the fireplace, sifting through letters. Suddenly he paused—"It's from him," he said. It was dated the day after my son's death, left off with my doorman.

A visceral surge shot through me as I grabbed the letter. And in an instant, I forgave him. Is there anyone whom you could not forgive? Forgave, not because he deserved to be forgiven, but because I wanted that passion back in my life. It was that passion that welded me to him.

In the fifteen years we knew each other, he never came into the room without a hard-on (hope that gives you a smile). It was *his* passion for me, that energy, that intensity that brought me alive again after my son's death.

I must give him credit. Once I saw him again he did everything he could to root me back into his life. "You don't know what it was like that night outside your building—ambulance—police—sirens. I couldn't get through." But you got through the crowds the night Bobby Kennedy was shot—close enough to take a close-up of his dead body, I wanted to say. But I didn't.

Whereas before he was undependable, he now did everything to let me know he was by my side. He would meet me outside New York Hospital, where I went every day to talk to Dr. John Mann, a suicide researcher, trying to understand my son's death. We walked in the park every day; he gave me a phone number where I could call him. In an animal way he instinctively knew how to be there for me. Treasuring things he said, I'd write them in my diary: "I love you"; "I'm afraid, I'm vulnerable in a way it's never happened to me before"; "I feel we've always been together. I want us to be in London together, go everywhere with me—I want us to have a history." We were sitting by the river, close, so close, and he said, "Kiss me, look at me. I'll never fail you." And later, "I'm so proud of you. I want to stand in front of you. Protect you."

I treasured the doodles he obsessed over on a pad by the phone when he checked his messages or in notes left on my pillow—drawings of his dachshund, whom he referred to as his "son" (he really doted on that dog), and I kept them along with other of his mementos, like a chip of the Berlin Wall, or a spray of heather in a painted lacquer box he brought me from Russia along with a sable fur hat. On these doodles of his "son" he'd scribble things like "I love you, I really do. I need you always—remember"; on another, "the day will be Sept. 19th," for that was to be the day the separation would take place. But when September 19 came around he would be in Istanbul or Timbuktu, and when he returned, our passion would burn dates out of the mind, and on and on it slipped into another month, another year, while the doodles kept piling up in the box.

Need I continue? Once Nancy Reagan was staying at my house and I was confiding in her my latest ups and downs with the Major. She knew him, had been photographed by him many times. We were giggling about something and Nancy said, "Let's call him." Of course I could never call him at home, so Nancy dialed the number.

When the Major's wife answered, she was most impressed: "Oh yes, Mrs. Reagan," she burbled, "yes—yes, he's right here." Nancy handed me the phone and there we were talking together. Ever after when Nancy came to visit she would point to my red phone and say, "That was the phone I made the call on!"

There were, of course, countless disappointments. Promises were broken. "Let's collaborate on a book," he said one day, "a book about Manhattan. My photographs, your text. We'll do it with a sharp edge." Why not? Swifty Lazar, my agent, swiftly arranged for publishers to meet us at my house. Agreements were made. There was much talk between me and the Major—over dinner or lunch, lying in bed, merrily egging each other on with ideas for the book. Finally, when the contract was sent to him to be signed, back it came unsigned, hand-delivered by his wife to Lazar's New York office—within the hour. I was furious, not only at the Major's irresponsible behavior, but because he had embarrassed me professionally. He didn't dare show his face after that for five weeks—but then one day he was back again as if nothing had happened. And, well, I *had* missed him . . .

From time to time he would say, "I don't want to lose you—you're not fed up with me, are you?" Oh no-no-no! I urgently reassured him. But fed up I should have been. Fed up with his attention span of a five-year-old, such as walking out on a movie ten minutes after it started if he didn't like it. Fed up with not being able to talk about a book I'd been reading. He favored only the tabloids, and every phone conversation usually started with, "What's the gossip?" Fed up with hearing about his "miserable marriage" and that he was going "to get a divorce." I was fed up, in fact, with everything except his passion for me.

Nothing new in all this, I suppose—but what gave him credibility was that there was none of the usual slinking around. At his suggestion we'd go to Le Cirque for dinner, to Elaine's for calamari. We were mentioned in gossip columns. He *loved* that. Twice we flew together to Swifty Lazar's Oscar Night party in Beverly Hills; he took me to Scotland to see his hometown and make a wish as we crossed the Brig O'Doon, the single-arch stone bridge built over the river Doon in the thirteenth century. Then on to Glasgow, where he impulsively ran into a bookstore and came back to present me with *The Complete Works of Robert Burns*. Later driving back to Troon, he stopped the car, got out, and filled my arms with heather and that evening placed a spray of it between the pages of Burns's poem "Tam O'Shanter," a poem about the bridge we had crossed that day, the bridge by which the Tam escaped from the witches and ghouls. "Heather is very, very lucky," he said. And he wrote in the book, "I stopped the car in front of Robert Burns' house, and you looked out. I told you how happy I was that you came to see my country. I will always remember it with fondest love." That was in the autumn. A few months later we were in London having high tea at Claridge's and when summer came we were together in Monte Carlo, where I had the delight of sewing a missing button onto his shirt.

And I'll have to tell you in all fairness—I wasn't faithful to him. Something instinctively told me I would be in real trouble if I cut myself off completely. But inevitably I'd be back with him. He made me laugh. He was crazy about me. It never occurred to me that he might be a fantast who believed the promises and things he said at the time he was saying them but who when the chips were down just couldn't follow through. As Clement Greenberg said of James Agee, he had "the ability to be sincere without being honest."

On and on it went, up and down the seesaw, until finally, thank God, I met someone else. Someone who wasn't married. I fell in love. And suddenly in a blink it was over . . . I know what you are thinking. How could you have put up with it for so long? Why did you? Why indeed? All my friends kept warning me not to believe what he said, for after all, his was the most clichéd line married men give to women they want to fool around with.

My son, Anderson Cooper, had no respect for the Major, and thought I was being self-destructive to take him seriously. But then it is one of my failings or strengths (however one perceives it) not to be suspicious of people. So for whatever it's worth—I tell you again—don't waste your time with married men. It really, truly, isn't worth the pain, the broken trust, the disappointment, over and over again. Will you listen? It depends. I think we are often attracted to and fall in love with those who remind us of the parent we are most obsessed with. For me it was my mother—elusive, unattainable, as was the Major. So to this day, I'm not sure I was really in love with him; it might have been that I was only attracted to the notion, the promise, that one day, someday, he would be mine.

He still calls from time to time. I have caller ID now, so I don't pick up. Recently, I ran in to him on the street. "You're the love of my life," he said. "I just couldn't start my life over again." For once, I knew he was telling the truth.

TWEEDLEDUM
AND TWEEDLEDEE

↦

When Johnny Carson saw the exhibit of my second
show of paintings and collages at the Hammer Gallery
in New York, he transformed his "Tonight" show into a
gallery and invited me to present them on television. The
night the show aired, Lewis Bloom saw it and the next
day called asking if I'd be interested in designing prints
for Bloomcraft fabrics. When they were produced, they
had a new look, whimsical and fresh, which took off like
a skyrocket and led to a future designing in all areas of
home furnishings. I was the first in the field to travel to
stores throughout the United States to launch my
collections and this time had the great good luck to have
the wonderful Pearl Bedell as my agent. My first venture
into fashion was designing scarves for Glentex. This
successful collection lured me into accepting Ben Shaw
when he proposed to back a Gloria Vanderbilt dress
business on Seventh Avenue.

The fashion business is fraught with romance, chance, glamour—very much like the theater. And because so much money is involved, it can, I was soon to discover, bring out terrible things in people. Yes, fashion is here today and gone tomorrow, not unlike a great flirt, but swept along not by the passion of love, but by passion for money and power. Fashion is a will-o'-the-wisp, a gaggle of red balloons held together by strings of gold. "Life's a beautiful thing as long as I hold the string, or I'd be a silly so-and-so if I should ever let her go," as my friend Harold Arlen sang in his song. Well, as it turned out, my red balloons were being yanked from the strings due to production problems, and my Seventh Avenue dress business was going belly-up. But not to worry. The day it flopped along came a marketing genius, Warren Hirsch, to the rescue, and a week later I found myself still on Seventh Avenue in an office right next to his in a company that manufactured blouses, and after huddling together, we came up with the idea of branching out into blue jeans that copied almost exactly the expensive ones I had found at Fiorucci's, only priced to "fly out of the store," as we say in the rag trade.

Then Warren came up with the idea of my doing TV commercials promoting the jeans. How to use my Stanislavsky acting training for this? But this fleeting concern soon vanished, and every week I'd be on the set with Kenneth doing my hair and Way Bandy doing my makeup, and even though I wasn't playing Ophelia, I was playing myself, and it was fun because it was a good product and I believed every pitch I made. Overnight, great piles of money started rolling in and everything was great.

That's the caviar part of the story, but all too soon Tweedledum and Tweedledee were waiting in the wings with nary a chocolate bar in sight, but that's coming—all too soon, so don't rush me.

There is nothing new under the sun, and so in fashion it's a matter of coming up with something that can be presented in a fresh way. The goal is always to catch the brass ring, hoping the timing turns it into gold. But it's not a marriage; it's a passing fancy, and most of the creativity involved is in projecting an aura, a style, a new interpretation that catches the imagination.

Oh, God—this is hard to write. At the height of my big success, my beloved husband, Wyatt Cooper, died unexpectedly of a heart attack. He was only fifty years old. My son Carter was twelve, Anderson ten. I hadn't been in therapy in years, but when I went for an annual checkup, I suddenly broke down and asked my doctor to recommend a therapist. She suggested a woman doctor and called New York Hospital. And although the doctor she named wasn't there, I could talk to someone else right away if I wanted.

I drove up to the entrance of Payne Whitney and there waiting on the steps stood a man in a white coat. He introduced himself as Dr. Zois and took me into the lobby of the hospital, where we sat talking as I tried to express my grief. Dr. Christ L. Zois was in his last year of medical school but appeared more like a high school student, a young Ryan O'Neal type, very personable and sensitive. When he went into practice, I became his first patient. I trusted him absolutely and completely, not only as my therapist but as my friend. I paid for him, his wife, and his son, along with his close friend, the lawyer Thomas A. Andrews, for a summer flight on the Concorde to France and on to Italy (the Gritti Palace in Venice, the Ritz in Paris). Frequently, they were guests at my house in Southampton, where Zois met Oona Chaplin (recently widowed) for the first time. She was so taken with him that he became her therapist too. I have no idea how much money he got from Oona, but it was a lot.

In 1989, Zois forged her name on a document in which she guaranteed repayment of a bank loan to him for $500,000. When he did not repay the loan, the bank tried to collect from Oona's estate on the guarantee, and the forgery was discovered. It seems that on the date in 1989 when she supposedly signed the guarantee, she was in a Swiss hospital, having suffered a stroke, and was unable to sign her name. Zois pleaded guilty to two counts of federal bank fraud, and somehow escaped going to jail by agreeing to make restitution to the bank involved. This is a matter of public record, as is everything else I am about to tell you. But I'm jumping ahead of my story.

Over the years, I gave Dr. Zois and his family, including his mother and Tom Andrews's mother, many presents—a Cartier watch, Tiffany silver, and so on. And of course I would recommend him to anyone who asked me for the name of a good therapist. One, Norma Kamali, became not only his patient, but also his lover.

Dr. Zois introduced me to Andrews and constantly urged me to make him my lawyer. But I never liked him, and besides, I already had a lawyer, Newman Lawler, and saw no reason to change. Then one day, while I was in conference with Mr. Lawler, something he said upset me, and I ran out and called Dr. Zois from a pay phone on the street.

"You see," he told me, "you need a lawyer like Tom Andrews; you're not tough enough for Seventh Avenue. I'll call him right now and you can go see him." Yes, and I went immediately to the office where Andrews worked. Afterward, I told Dr. Zois again that I still didn't like Andrews. (Oona never did, either, but followed her instinct

It Seemed Important at the Time

and never took him as her lawyer despite Dr. Zois's urging.) "Never mind," he said, "I'll be there as buffer." And buffer he was. Buffer as I gave Andrews power of attorney and control of my bank accounts, buffer as I made him my business manager, buffer as I put up with his abrasive manner and boorish ways. I trusted him, because I trusted my therapist, Dr. Zois. He sent me papers to sign—legalese I found hard to understand—which I didn't read because I trusted him.

Dr. Zois presented, with great authority, imaginary scenarios for dealing with various situations. "Do this," he'd say, "and they'll do that." What he didn't tell me was a scenario that he and Andrews were plotting on their own. Unknown to me, they had formed a fifty-fifty partnership, A to Z Associates, which received all of the legal fees and commissions on my licensing income that I believed were being paid to Andrews alone. Apart from the deception involved, it was unethical for a lawyer to share fees with a nonlawyer, and equally unethical for a medical doctor to have business dealings with a patient. Worse, Andrews used his authority over my bank accounts to write large checks to Dr. Zois for "retainer fees" and other fictitious purposes, and to himself for personal expenses.

But stealing from my bank accounts did not satisfy them for long. They had a bigger plan.

Andrews called urgently; there were papers I must

Gloria Vanderbilt

sign immediately for tax reasons. They were coming over by messenger, who would wait while I signed. Licenses to use my name were being put under one "umbrella" to be called "Gloria Concepts Inc."

"No," I said, "I don't like the name."

"Forget it," he said. "There's no time to change it."

The messenger arrived soon after, and because I trusted Dr. Zois, I signed a lot of papers as usual without reading them. What I was signing, it turned out, gave 50 percent of the shares of Gloria Concepts Inc. to A to Z Associates. In the same way, Andrews got me to grant Gloria Concepts Inc. an exclusive, perpetual license to use my name in the sale of all kinds of home furnishings, and then to sell my remaining 50 percent interest in Gloria Concepts Inc. to a partnership called Design Management Partners, which was nothing but a front for Andrews and Dr. Zois. They later sold Gloria Concepts to a woman in Florida.

By these means, Andrews and Dr. Zois swindled me out of my name and home furnishings license, and much money, and because Andrews had not paid my taxes, the Internal Revenue Service came in and took my house, my apartment—everything.

Andrews and Dr. Zois counted on my never having the guts to question what they had done to me. In any legal proceeding against them, I would have to sign away the doctor/patient confidence, and Dr. Zois could then make up anything about me that he wanted to.

Strange, after all those years how little Dr. Zois knew me. I may look fragile, but I'm no Humpty-Dumpty. Although I was knocked flat, it would take more than that to knock me off the wall. Later, through friends, I went to attorney Jerome K. Walsh and he restored my faith in the legal profession by bringing Dr. Christ L. Zois and Thomas A. Andrews before the medical and bar association disciplinary committees. After prolonged hearings, Zois and Andrews were disbarred from the medical and legal professions for what they had done to me.

In court, I won a judgment against them for $1.6 million, only the tip of the iceberg of what they had stolen, but I have yet to get one penny of it. Before dying of cancer, Andrews liquidated his assets into cash, moved the cash to God-knows-where, moved with his partner-wife to Florida, and left a bankrupt estate. Zois is left a convicted felon, stripped of his medical license, and last I heard he was bankrupt in New Jersey, living off his son.

My friend Bill Blass, like a knight in shining armor, supported me until I got on my feet and started life all over again, with shows of paintings and collages, designing, writing books, and—in love (as always!). Best of all, I have my health, my energy, and I'm still dancing on my tippy-toes.

So who wins? I'll leave it to you.

Gloria Vanderbilt

ANOTHER PART OF THE FOREST

It was at this point, after I lost everything (except my secret heart), that I decided perhaps it was time to get involved with someone for security's sake. Carol Marcus Saroyan was now married to Walter Matthau, whose closest friend and gambling partner was David Begelman, a big-shot producer and entrepreneur. He was someone they thought I should meet.

"He's quite rich," Carol oohed excitedly, and a little dinner party was arranged at his house before one of their poker nights.

Oh dear—well, I really wasn't too taken with him. It wasn't just his porcineness, it was the pretentiousness I didn't cotton to. But you know, with my imagination I can flip-flop and slant things optimistically. And so I did.

Begelman lived in one of those huge houses referred to in Beverly Hills as "lovely homes," filled with artwork, obviously wildly expensive and up-to-the-moment but lacking any personal meaning. Dinner was served by a staff out of central casting, and soon after coffee was poured Carol and I left, while Walter stayed on for the poker night. Host David escorted us ceremoniously down the long hallway, pausing to point out his acquisitions on either side while I murmured polite nothings—"Yes, lovely shadows in that," and so on. But could I sincerely think of this man in my life? I had heard about some check-forging activities he'd been involved in; was it only gossip, perhaps? Certainly Carol and Walter and their crowd in Beverly Hills thought highly of him and stood staunchly behind him. Later that night in the Beverly Wilshire Hotel I mulled this over as I lay unable to sleep, and came to a decision—no, in the long run I wouldn't be able to bring it off.

But still I went back to the East Coast thinking about him. Hard not to, as he called often, at odd hours during the day, usually from a car on the way to one meeting or another. In his voice was immediacy, impulsiveness, the energy of big things going on, exciting things happening, and that was attractive.

Mary Lazar called—"This is very exciting!"— intimating that we would soon be a couple. But exciting to whom? Not to me, who still irreverently and secretly viewed him as Porky Pig. Did I want to be a "we" with David Begelman? Sensing my withdrawal, he flew to New York, suggesting dinner at Le Cirque.

Maybe he *was* rich. But no matter how rich—
was it worth it? And worth what? The price to be paid:
pretending to feel something I didn't, pretending I was
somebody I wasn't. Luxury can cushion you; it's seductive
to sink into, wallow in, but after a while you become so
accustomed to it that you forget it's even there, and you

IT SEEMED IMPORTANT AT THE TIME

long for something to replace it, something real, something to love.

"Come to London with me? And Paris?" he asked. "After this trip you and I together will know everything there is to know in the whole wide world." That's pretty intriguing. Yes, oh yes! "Follow your heart, follow your heart," he kept saying, nodding sagely, and to make sure I got the message, he wrote it on the cards with the flowers he sent—a steady stream of them.

I was following my heart, only it wasn't leading in his direction. If the truth were known, I really couldn't imagine rolling around in the feathers with him, much less wanting to discover together "everything there is to know in the whole wide world." Sounded interesting, but not with him. Being alone with him was difficult, too. After the dinner at Le Cirque, going to that what's-its-name club in the basement of the Sherry-Netherland that he was so snooty about being a member of, what was there to talk about?

Best to dance, and soon we were on our feet, swinging and swaying to "Love Is Here to Stay," as he kept trying to gaze into my eyes, mumbling words to the George Gershwin song—"It's very clear, our love is here to stay . . ." (Not with you, I wanted to scream.) But every time our eyes met, his would skittishly shift away. I looked at the place on his forehead between his eyes (promise, it

Gloria Vanderbilt

works), which makes it appear as though you're making eye contact, and said, "It's sleepy time down south, David, let's call it a day."

". . . day, yes day, not for a year, but ever and a day."

He twirled faster around the dance floor. But later in the limo he sunk into a petulant mood, staring out at the glittery lights of the city, and once again there was nothing to say to each other.

Could he have thought I was the millionairess of his dreams, the answer to his gambling and credibility problems, at the same time I thought of him as the millionaire of *my* dreams, the answer to security for me and my children? If so—*oy vey,* did we both meet the wrong vampires.

Later, plagued with gambling debts and who knows what else, he killed himself in a suite in the Century Plaza Towers in Century City, which is the old back lot of Twentieth Century–Fox, after a final assignation with his mistress at the time, Sandy Bennett, the ex-wife of Tony Bennett. He left twenty farewell notes.

SUBSTITUTES

Traveling recently with a friend, as we were sitting waiting to board the plane, she asked, "Who was the love of your life?"

Without thinking I said, "The man I love right now." Then as I thought about it later I wondered if that was really true, and came to the conclusion that it *was* true, but at the same time, it *wasn't*.

To answer truthfully I would have to say that the

love of my life was my mother. My search for love has and always will be to revive the dream of fulfilling the half-forgotten, inevitably frustrated wishes for perfect harmony and complete mutuality— wishes that originated in the now-buried fantasy

of obtaining the perfect mother to love me unerringly and unceasingly. And although I accept that it was not in her nature to ever be capable of this, the longing is so deep in *my* nature that I have to constantly resist being drawn to men and situations to once again replay the old scenario, always believing that this time the fairy tale will have a happy ending. The men are substitutes, let's say, substitutes for my old sweetheart.

HAZEL KELLY

In a garden I lean down and look into a flower, so close the drops of dew blur my eyes. Absorbed into joy, I become the petals. Yes, I tend to idealize and romanticize even the simplest moments of daily life, so you can imagine what I do when it comes to romantic love, which is by definition an act of imagination.

Beauty and joy come unexpectedly, always when we're not looking for them. It's there in colors and the delight they provide. It's in the fabrics we wear, the varying textures, the cut and shape that transform them, giving them the beauty to attract. It's in fabrics for a room, in colors for walls to paint a house of dreams that exists only in fantasy. In the scent of lilacs, dew-drenched in sunlight. In phosphorescent light from the moon on waves as we walk along the beach. In making love on a Sunday afternoon with the sound of rain on the roof. In snow falling with shadows hurrying past. In the joy of being alone, walking in a world where everything is white, pure, the cold, fast-falling flakes melting on my face.

Gloria Vanderbilt

A kaleidoscope suddenly turns and another pattern forms into a design not seen before. Is it enough? Do you want it to be, when with another twist you can transform the kaleidoscope into something else, the colors different, muted perhaps—peaceful? But be careful what you wish for, because it's likely you'll find it. It's what you do with it after that matters, but that's another story. Still, there's sure to be someone waiting in the wings. That someone might even be yourself.

Think about visiting a city you've never been in before. There is something strangely fulfilling about going alone into a café, ordering scrambled eggs and bacon, coffee, a muffin; something about it that is calm and secret. No one knows where you are or who you are, and no one cares. It is a completely free and independent moment, and demands nothing of you except for you to be yourself. Which brings me to Hazel Kelly.

It was a misty day and I was hurrying along on Park Avenue, people rushing by. Suddenly a man passing said, "Miss?" and as I turned toward the stranger, he said, "Are you Hazel Kelly?" I shook my head. "Oh, sorry," he said, and hurried by.

It happened so quickly, but when a few seconds later I turned back to find him, he had disappeared into the crowd. What if I had said, "Yes" . . . what would have happened? Had I done this, it would have fit in with one of my deepest fantasies, which is to get on a bus without asking its destination, and then get off in an unknown town, find a job there, take on a new identity—becoming someone else, becoming Hazel Kelly. Why not? Who is she? What made this man think I was her? Maybe he'll read this someday and I'll find out.

SOMEONE LIKE YOU

Now it's time to tell you about the long, lanky, very tall, very dry lemon I mentioned before I started telling you about the Fantast.

"So baby Dahl's after you," my snappy *Vogue* editor friend said. I smiled at this description of the six-foot-four-something whom I was running out to meet at the Central Park Zoo. "That's what they called Roald Dahl when he was in the RAF," she went on, as I merrily waved good-bye.

On this lovely day we were to meet where the seals frolicked, and I was afraid he wouldn't wait even if I was a second late, because when he suggested this rendezvous I had been vague about encouraging it, and he may have decided I wasn't going to show up. I hastened down the steps at the 66th Street entrance to Central Park, and as I turned the corner, there he was in the distance, with his back toward me, leaning against the railing, looking at the seals as they slithered in and out of the water, in and out and up onto the rocks.

I paused—he hadn't seen me. I could turn, go back up the steps, and never see him again. Better cut out now, quick, I decided, but just as I did, he turned and saw me, and instead of running out, I ran into his arms—and into big trouble.

Roald Dahl had recently married the actress Patricia Neal, and she was in Chicago doing a play, *The Children's Hour,* and as you know I never get involved with married men, so what was I doing with him? Well, nothing. We could be friends, couldn't we?

Yes, but there was something about it that somehow wasn't like that. From the minute I met him at a party, he had singled me out. He was lofty, opinionated, condescending to everyone else, so he considered his attention to me to be quite a favor, as I was soon to discover. He had that attitude so many of the English have toward Americans. I don't think many of them really like us. They're fascinated, but in that love/hate way. Yes, he was full of himself, and ripe with the recent success of his short stories, which had appeared in *The New Yorker* and were now in a book titled *Someone Like You* that everyone in town was talking about.

I took note that someone like him was interested in someone like me. I knew it even more the next day when he called and asked when we could see each other. We'd had an intense discussion at the party about painting, and he was interested in seeing my work, so there he was at my studio having tea and crumpets and more discussions about art with me.

The next day he went on a book tour and didn't call, but then a letter came. My heart went pitty-pat the first time I saw the unknown handwriting with my name on the envelope because I knew it was from him. Although we hadn't even kissed yet, in the letter he wrote of walking down a street in Houston, imagining I was with him and stopping under a tree to kiss. I was very taken with the way he put it—well, he was a writer after all— but I started getting scared about how I would feel if I saw him again. There were more letters, and then he was

back in New York and I was on my way to the zoo again and the seals and the big trouble.

He had very definite opinions about everything, and I'd nod sympathetically, although I didn't agree with most of it. He wasn't crazy about Americans, as I said, but he intimated that his condescending attitude didn't include me. Why did this seem somehow insidiously flattering? Of course he wanted to go to bed and I did too, but we didn't. I kept it simmering, like a teenager under a curfew, because I was scared that if we did go to bed I'd really be lost, lost, lost because . . . because . . .

Then he surprised me by showing me manuscripts of his stories written in his own sacred hand. "You select the one you like," he suggested.

The one I selected hadn't been published—*that* impressed him. Maybe he thought I'd be like all the other pushy Americans and choose "Someone Like You" just because it was the famous one and the title of his book. He took me to Marchi's to celebrate, and over a glass of wine handed me the pages. They were held together by a thread, and hanging from the thread was a gold charm— a greyhound, an antique key to wind a fob watch. Oh the thrill of the loved one's gift. No matter what, how big or small, it assumes magic powers of a relic (how strange later when unexpectedly I came upon it in a drawer and found it meant nothing at all to me). It throbbed with

Gloria Vanderbilt

signs and portents. What did it mean? Up and down I went, yes-no-yes-no. The bouquet of daisies he sent me—can you believe it—I went through the lot, plucking off each petal—he loves me/he loves me not.

But wait—things *were* happening. Just before his wife came back from Chicago, he invited me to the apartment they were living in on the West Side opposite the Museum of Natural History. I was tempted, but hesitated—don't, don't open that door. But I did and found myself as I knew I would, an intruder drawn into the intimacy of their life—the wedding picture on a table, a robe just my size hanging on a peg, on another table lay mail—her name on it—the picture of a woman smiling in a silver frame . . . her mother? His mother? He had talked to me once about his "old mother." Eerie seeing their bed (king size) with the flowered sheets, but it was even more eerie when he tried to pull me into it, even though he knew I wasn't going to comply.

"Come, there's something I'd like to show you." He sat down behind the desk and took a black leather jewel box out of the drawer, talking, in that slow way he had, about what was inside, how rare and exquisite it was, how he spotted it in James Robinson's and knew it was *exactly* what he'd been looking for, on and on, as I sat melting like a piece of butter in the sun, because I knew it was for me. "Open it." He handed me the box, and inside on black velvet sat a plump little enameled Victorian pansy pin, purple and yellow as could be with a twinkly diamond in the center. Breathlessly I held it in the palm of my hand. "Oh, Roald, I, I . . . ."

"Do you think Pat will like it?"

I smiled quickly, nodding oh yes, yes, and we went out onto the street and walked together for a few minutes. He seemed to be having trouble breathing—well, it is hard to squeeze juice out of a dry lemon—"You're the— finest—person I've ever—known—but . . . ."

"She's going to love it," I said again, turning fast, walking away and leaving him on the sidewalk, walking fast across the park toward home.

Many years later, when Pat Neal was in the midst of divorcing Roald Dahl, I invited her to our house in Southampton for a weekend. At dinner on Saturday night she was wearing the pansy pin. I didn't mention I had seen it before. Apparently Roald had told her about me when she got back to New York after the play closed. How I'd pursued him while she was away, but he resisted— you get the gist. I did too but I let it go, slip by. As my Irish nanny Dodo used to say, "Sometimes it's best to leave it where Jesus flings it."

FUN

⬌

As Dorothy Parker once said, "There's nothing more fun than a man."

Remember fun? Sometimes we forget. Fun is not some earthshaking meeting with—or thinking you've met—the Other, the *it* of your life. Fun is being with someone who makes you feel like a girl, makes you feel girly. Even Maureen Dowd must have girly moments (sometimes?). And what about Hillary Clinton? She deserves such moments more than any of us. We all *should* have, *must* have, *have to have* fun now and then, if for no other reason than to lessen the burden of our secret hearts.

Let me tell you about the artist René Bouché. Wow, did he know how to make a girl feel girly. An artist in love with you will paint your portrait, obsess with every nuance, every turn of your head, every eyelash out of place, notice *everything* about you, be there for you in ways so thoughtful even you with your feminine sensitivity haven't even thought of, like phoning you on the dot of

143
⬌

seven in case your alarm hadn't gone off. Do you like that idea or would it drive you nuts?

I met René when he did a drawing of me for *Vogue*. Later I found out that he had served with the French Army, been captured by the Germans, escaped into the south of France, and been brought to America by Condé Nast. But what really impressed me was how after being rejected by *Vogue* editor Edna Chase, he trained himself in six weeks to develop a fresh new technique, drawings done on blotting paper, soft easy lines that created a new trend in fashion. He went on to become *Vogue*'s star illustrator—all without ever having lost belief in himself as an artist.

After having gone through the agonizing self-consciousness of my teen years, I had said good-bye to all that, and had accepted that whatever I had in the way of looks worked OK for me. However, René's reaction to whatever it was I had made me feel extra girly indeed. Short and virile, he brought to mind Picasso's drawings of satyrs—yes, definitely—with eyes that held centuries of intelligence behind them. The desperate intensity as he attacked the canvas, the groans and grunts as if the brushstrokes were darts being thrown at a target . . . Who could resist? Not I, said the little brown hen. Quelle aphrodisiac! It blew me away—away, out of the window of his studio overlooking Central Park, straight out over the green trees, onward, up, up, up up. And I knew that soon, very soon . . . Oh goody—fun ahead!

After that first drawing for *Vogue,* there was another (not for *Vogue*) and another and another. He saw me as two people—one tender and fragile, the other strong and determined. Between discovering one and the other, he'd drive us to places in the country for dinner, to inns I had no idea existed. It was like being on holiday in Europe, only I was being adored and pampered right here in my own backyard. He called me his Heavenly Creature, but then he had a list of other Heavenly Creatures too.

It Seemed Important at the Time

High on his list was the aloof Marietta Tree, and then there was the sexy nymphet, Bee Whistler Dabney. But I wasn't jealous because I wasn't in love with him—you know, in *that* way. I was, however, in love with his passion and love of beauty, and with how he had mastered the art of living. He had superb taste in everything—nothing in his life lacked perfection. The quirky root chair and off-center placement of the sofa in his studio, a table holding the ivory figure of a naked woman. Physicians in ancient China had used such a figure for shy patients to point to the spot that hurts. Certainly nothing was hurting me, but was I starting to hurt him? Is there anyone you feel you may have hurt? Surely there must be.

I hate that feeling and kept thinking about another time, when a man said to me in a taxi as we sped to the airport on an impulsive escape to Jamaica, "Make sure you mean this, don't bring out the wildebeest." What he was really saying was don't unlock the secret heart unless you mean it. I didn't have to answer; all he did was look at me, and he told the taxi to turn back. We never saw each other again as lovers—only friends. Always try to keep lovers as friends—they shouldn't ever be strangers—they can't be anyway.

Everything with René had been fun, an act of high spirits—until that wildebeest popped into it. He was serious when the only thing I was serious about was my acting career, which he didn't take seriously at all. I didn't want to hurt him, yet maybe I already had. And then I started rehearsing for a play, drifting away more and more—you know, getting a crush on my leading man, things like that. And the more I drifted the more he started holding on tight. Finally there was a nasty scene, a knock, knock, knocking on my door after opening night, and it wasn't fun anymore. But oh, what fun it had been while it lasted. And we did remain friends.

IT SEEMED IMPORTANT AT THE TIME

QUITE BY CHANCE

Leopold had sailed on the *Queen Mary* to England, where he would conduct the London Philharmonic Orchestra, and then be off to conduct at La Scala in Milan; I was to have gone on the tour with him. But two days before sailing I came down with the most nasty sore throat, which turned into a head cold—so there he was on the high seas and here was I in bed with lots of Kleenex, feeling miserable, yet somehow secretly relieved that I hadn't been able to travel, even though I had looked forward to being in Europe with Leopold. He was always happier there, freer in his spirit, and that made me feel closer to him.

Anyway, there I was sneezing away when a call came from Rosemary Warburton, who was chairman of the April in Paris annual charity ball. Ah, these tempests in teapots: Rosie was quite beside herself because Audrey Hepburn—who was to have played Lafayette in a tableau staged at the ball, with Broadway producer Gilbert Miller presenting himself as Benjamin Franklin—had come

Gloria Vanderbilt

down with sniffles, and would I, could I, step in and take her place?

Destiny once again was tapping me on the shoulder. I roused myself from the sickbed and lickety-splitted it over to the Waldorf ballroom where rehearsal was taking place. I fit right into the tableau vivant, and by the evening of the ball, a few days later, my sore throat had completely disappeared and there I was making an entrance in a General Lafayette costume with Gilbert Miller by my side, whispering, "Have you ever thought of being on the stage?" Can you believe it—that's exactly what he said. Only you will know that he picked the very words right out of my secret heart.

I was so stunned I did nothing. Then a few days later, while walking on Fifth Avenue, I told a friend about this amazing event and she looked at me and said, "Why don't you call him—take him up on it—see what he says?"

We were passing a phone booth, and impulsively I took a coin out of my purse, went in, closed the door, and did just that. It seemed Miller *was* serious, and the next day I found myself in his office talking about Ferenc Molnar's play *The Swan*. Quick as a wink a production was in the works, a tryout at Rowena Stevens's Pocono Playhouse. *Life* magazine wanted to photograph me in the costume I was to wear in the play, so there I was, all dressed up in a lace dress designed in 1910 by Worth of

Paris, waiting on my terrace at Ten Gracie Square for *Life*
photographer Gordon Parks to show up. And show up he
did—right on the dot.

When I start describing Gordon, I find myself
hard-put to come up with the right words because I'd like
to present him to you dashing through the door as I saw
him that first day. He was so warm, gifted with innate
style and grace, someone so completely at ease in his skin,
so completely genuine and sincere—the real thing.

I have to digress here and give you a sense of
what it was like growing up in a world of bigotry, where
my Whitney relatives referred to Jews as *les juifs,* and my
mother, who had many Jewish friends, more tolerantly
used to smile and say affectionately, "Oh, we all have our
favorite Jew." And later even Leopold was amused to tell
the "joke" about a Frenchman who hears mention of "the
chosen people," and the response *quelle drôle de goût*
(what strange taste). Blacks were referred to as "colored
people," if referred to at all. Once I even heard Aunt
Gertrude's Irish cook refer to blacks as "having the curse
of Cain upon them." In New York City in the '30s and
'40s you rarely saw a black person on the streets unless
you went to Harlem. In movies they were parodied by
"Stepnfetchit" or Hattie McDaniel playing the "colored"
maid. Later, when one of Leopold's daughters married a
Jew, he said, "What's she going to do, live in a ghetto?"

Gordon Parks was the first black person I ever had the opportunity to come close to, much less get to know. And from the moment we met right up to this very day, there never were nor ever have been any boundaries between us. We became friends instantly. I felt, I *know* this person. By now most of us admire his extraordinary achievements as photographer, writer (*The Learning Tree* is read in classrooms across America), his work directing films, including *Shaft*, his orchestral symphonies, fifty-one—or more—doctorates from such universities as Princeton and Harvard, which I (also a high school dropout) especially appreciate. I can only imagine what it must have been like for him through the years, growing up amid prejudice. Yet his book *Choice of Weapons* tells

us how he chose to fight bigotry. His weapon? Love. No doubt the strong support of his mother gave him this strength of character and his ability to love without being afraid.

I have been photographed by many—Richard Avedon, Louise Dahl-Wolfe, Tony Frissell, Horst, George Hurrell, Hoyningen-Huene, Annie Leibovitz, Cecil Beaton, and so on—and it's always fascinating to experience each in a different way. The photographer *tells* you, transmits to you what he sees, what he wants, and it's fun to become litmus paper and give it to him. Avedon's genius is a great example of this, and Gordon brings his gentle sensitivity, a love of beauty that comes from his spirit, and it merges into yours. Today his photographs are continuously exhibited in touring shows all around the world, and photographs he took of me that day on the terrace are a part of this exhibit, bringing back that day we first met.

It's almost inconceivable now to imagine how surprising it was in the 1950s for us to be seen together, simply because he was black and I was white. It was almost impossible then to move freely without drawing attention to our friendship, often in a negative way. But for us the issue just didn't exist and we never wasted a minute talking about it.

Now it's 2004, and the day after we drove to have dinner with our Princeton friends. Today I received a fax

Gloria Vanderbilt

from Joyce Carol Oates in which she said, "It was so very touching to see you and Gordon holding hands. . . . The two of you have acquired a sort of iconic significance. You are both strikingly attractive in the most obvious, immediate sense, and then in a more ethereal/mythic sense. Your rather creamy skin, and Gordon's cocoa-skin; your slender black clothing, and Gordon's dapper powder-grey wide-lapel suit, his natty black-and-white shoes about to break into a tap-dance."

Often the best things that happen come quite by chance, unexpectedly, as my meeting with Gordon did. We've known each other through years of good times, bad times (we both lost sons), and times in between. Gordon is always there for me, as I am for him. There is nothing in the world I couldn't tell him that he wouldn't understand—he is a true friend. I love him dearly.

"Don't you think it's about time we got married?" Now and then over the years he says this to me. As always, I smile, pat his hand, and say, "But darling, we already are."

IT SEEMED IMPORTANT AT THE TIME

WHAT ARE YOU GOING TO WEAR?

⟨—⟩

Lf you wanted to look very sexy, how would you dress? This is the question I kept asking myself as I started packing for a weekend trip to meet *him* in Chicago. To me, sexy evokes receptiveness, an awareness of self, an attitude of confidence mixed with a slight edgy indecisiveness that could go one way or the other. A certain reserve also has allure, but it has to be tempered with warmth; otherwise it doesn't work. Color is important (don't wear orange), but even more important is the fabric—plushy, soft, nothing scratchy or prickly. Think of touching moss, slightly moist, but warm from the sun. How it feels on you is how it will feel to him when he hugs you, and it will make him want to hug you again.

From the moment he sets eyes on me, I want to have immediate appeal, style, and charm—but I want to be a sexpot too. Why not? Blue velvet is perfect, the very thing. But that's for later—dinner, squashy apricot roses

Gloria Vanderbilt

in a silver vase, on a white linen table lit by candlelight, champagne in fluted crystal, the Ritz in Paris, "I kiss your hand, Madame," and so on.

He has arranged everything about the weekend. The key to the room will be waiting at the Drake, at the desk, in my name. I'm to call him when I'm ensconced. Just thinking about it leaves me weak and trembling.

I keep looking at myself in the mirror to remember what I look like. My imagination runs wild. It's the first reencounter since our first meeting and I'm swept away by my own imagination. As I look at my face in the mirror, I'm trying to remember what *his* face looks like. Over and over again, I review that first meeting in my mind. Like an old movie reel, it plays itself over again, each time cut, spliced, and edited according to the need of the moment.

That fateful day, what I was wearing was anything but sexy—a navy sweater, long skirt, and boots. Replaying the scene in my mind, the sweater is pale gray, cashmere fitted gently, held in at the waist with a silvered coin

IT SEEMED IMPORTANT AT THE TIME

belt; the skirt is short, and the shoes, spiky torture Manolo Blahniks I'd never dream of wearing.

He had come to my studio to see my work. The friend who was with him talked all the time. *He* hardly said anything. Dark and shut in himself, passive, distant. If we'd been alone, we would have ended up in each other's arms. When they left I thought, That's that, I'll never see him again. But then he called, and now here I am on my way to Chicago. I like a man who takes charge, isn't passive. Last night I fell asleep early, lapsing into a deep sudden sleep, and in my dream I came to him, all of me coming to him in waves, as if I were part of a great ocean, and the waves were breaking one on top of the other as they reached him, warm waves (not cold as the sea sometimes is), and I came over and over again, and woke to find myself feeling delicious, with the comforter over me in the cold of the night. For a long time I lay dazed and happy, turned inside out, and my hand still wet with the taste of the sea. I wonder if I'll ever feel close enough to tell him about this? Maybe not. Best wear my red beret and flashy smile. It's so easy when you don't give a damn.

Gloria Vanderbilt

LONG DISTANCE

⟷

I walk from my house onto the street, and stop under a tree to look down at a sea of autumn leaves, yellow and gleaming from the rain with an intensity that takes my breath away. The street is empty, and I stand there a long time, my eyes expanding to hold on to the yellow brilliance. It's a different yellow from the remembered yellow of my mother's velvet dress, but it reminds me of it nonetheless; it reminds me—as so many things often do—of her.

I lean down and pick up a leaf, fold it into my handkerchief. Later I'll look at it again and throw it away. Make of that whatever you will. Right now the boundaries of myself are changing. Is it because I'm in love again and the spring is coming? I'm in love again and my heart strings are strumming (what is the name of that song?). Whatever it is, it's autumn, and spring is a long way off. We have coldhearted winter to get through first—the north winds shall blow, and we will have snow, and what will robin do then, poor thing, what will robin do then? Well, this robin will be in love. Right now it's with an ocean of yellow leaves on a black pavement wet with rain. All day long as I walk around the city I'll be seeing that yellow in my head, thinking of *him*. Actually I think of him more than I see him, because he lives in Chicago and here I am in New York. It requires a balancing act to remain on that line and creates a tension that is extremely pleasurable but potentially problematic.

I think of him a lot, projecting myself into wondering what he's doing right now this minute. I'm about to submerge my identity in the Other. Is the balancing act worth it? All my friends tell me how lucky I am to have distance between us—why, you could keep on going for years and years, they tell me—with your temperament you need space and solitude for your work. Actually they have a point—I'm always thrilled when he's coming to visit and equally thrilled when he leaves. There are things about him and about me that might get on each other's nerves if we lived together. There's the fitful insomnia that means he can't sleep in the same bed as the beloved—no cuddling, no big toe in the night to connect with. He's high-strung, too suspicious to really trust anyone, too edited to allow spontaneity. He tends to measure out his life with coffee spoons, loves schedules, sets of "rules" (I hate "rules"), likes only junk food, sinks into the quicksand of a moody distant silence—*unreachable*—I could go on and on . . .

Still, when all's said and done, he is the Nijinsky of cunnilingus. What more can a girl want? We can't have everything—oh, but we can try—we can try.

EPILOGUE

⟺

Dear Others—you who are not mentioned in this romance memoir—do I hear a sigh of relief? Rest easy, you will always remain in my secret heart brightly twinkling.

I hope that some of this has brought a few smiles into your life. As for the tears, they're mine alone.

Life isn't a cabaret, and when I hear someone singing "Is that all there is? Is that all there is?" I want

⟺

Gloria Vanderbilt

to shout Yes! Goddamn it, that's all there is and it's damn jolly good enough.

It's *more* than jolly good enough, the miracle to be reborn with each day, the miracle of each night to descend into the darkness of dreams and wake into the new day. It may be the day you fall in love with a tree, a flower, a face you see passing by in a taxi, a change in the weather. It's the miracle of the hour as day turns into night, and you turn on the radio and unexpectedly hear a song that brings back a memory of happiness so clearly that you are right back there when it happened. It may be the smell of bread baking, or a cake of soap as you unwrap it. Today may even be the day you meet someone who will change your life, and this time it might last for a very long time. Why not? Dreams sometimes do come true.

PHOTOGRAPHY CREDITS

◆────◆

©Bill Cunningham: iv–v

Library of Congress, Prints & Photographs Division,
Toni Frissell Collection: 2, 95, 135, 160

Photography Collection, Harry Ransom Humanities
Research Center, The University of Texas at Austin: 7

© Bettmann/Corbis: 12

Gloria Vanderbilt Private Collection: 17, 29, 33, 37, 44, 47,
52, 55, 59, 67, 80, 83, 86, 98, 111, 123, 132, 133, 157

Karsh/Camera Press/Retna: 38

Frances McLaughlin-Gill/ Courtesy of *Harper's Bazaar*: 61

Estate of W. Eugene Smith/Blackstar: 70

© Gordon Parks: 73, 92

Library of Congress, Prints & Photographs Division, Look Magazine
Photograph Collection, Gloria Vanderbilt Private Collection: 75

Paul Schutzer/Time Life Pictures/Getty Images: 89

© *New York Post*/McCarten: 101

© Cris Alexander: 102

Wyatt Cooper: 105

Anderson Cooper: 129

© 2004 Milton H. Greene Archives Inc.
www.archivesmhg.com: 139

© Jack Rosen: 144

Roddy McDowall: 147

Jeanne Wilmot Carter: 151

Aaron Shikler ©: 155